HEALTH CARE ISSUES, COSTS AND ACCESS

ACHIEVING THE QUADRUPLE AIM IN A TECHNOLOGY-DRIVEN TRANSFORMED HEALTH SYSTEM

BETTER CARE, IMPROVED HEALTH, LOWER COSTS AND DECREASED MEDICAL LIABILITY

HEALTH CARE ISSUES, COSTS AND ACCESS

Additional books in this series can be found on Nova's website under the Series tab.

Additional e-books in this series can be found on Nova's website under the e-book tab.

HEALTH CARE ISSUES, COSTS AND ACCESS

ACHIEVING THE QUADRUPLE AIM IN A TECHNOLOGY-DRIVEN TRANSFORMED HEALTH SYSTEM

BETTER CARE, IMPROVED HEALTH, LOWER COSTS AND DECREASED MEDICAL LIABILITY

JAMES B. COUCH, M.D., J.D., FACPE
SENIOR PHYSICIAN EXECUTIVE
JHD GROUP, INC.

nova publishers
New York

For permission to use material from this book please contact us:
Telephone 631-231-7269; Fax 631-231-8175
Web Site: http://www.novapublishers.com

Library of Congress Cataloging-in-Publication Data

ISBN: 978-1-63321-675-4

Library of Congress Control Number: 2014946526

Published by Nova Science Publishers, Inc. † New York

I dedicate this book to my loving wife, Maryann,
and our three wonderful children, John, Katherine and Laura,
to whom I shall gladly pass the torch soon, as they embark
on their own lives and careers.

CONTENTS

PREFACE

In speaking with physicians around the country, a common lament heard is that the current healthcare financing system makes it very difficult to achieve the Triple Aim. The goals of the Triple Aim are to deliver better care to improve individual and population health at lower costs. Although it has always been physicians' intent to deliver better care to restore, improve and maintain the health of their patients, doing so with lower costs, also, has been particularly difficult, in a healthcare financing system which has actually penalized this accomplishment.

Even for those physicians (and other practitioners) who have been successful in achieving the Triple Aim, there was always the specter of increased medical liability risk. Our medical liability system has evolved hand in glove with the fee for service reimbursement system to create the mythology that "more care is better care". So, if "more care is better care", practicing cost effectively by doing less, but achieving more, still could put such physicians (and other practitioners) at medico-legal risk. Should unexpectedly bad patient outcomes occur, plaintiffs' attorneys would argue that these would not have occurred if those physicians and others had done more to diagnose and/or treat their clients. This is why achieving the fourth goal of the "Quadruple Aim" (decreasing the risks and actualities of medical liability), at least in our current healthcare financing and liability system, has been so difficult.

This book does not provide any "silver bullets" concerning how to achieve the Quadruple Aim. However, it does seek to demonstrate how a more technology-driven, value based financing and delivery system, with fairer methods for resolving medical injury disputes, may help the U.S. achieve the four goals of the Quadruple Aim much more easily than is currently possible.

As the country transitions from a volume to a value based system for reimbursement, we have a real opportunity to change our "more care if better care" mindset. Along with the transparency movement in healthcare spurred by healthcare reform and the new approaches to medical injury dispute resolution detailed in Chapter 8, there is a real chance to address both the "conspiracy of silence" and the "lottery mindset" that has characterized our current medical liability system. In a value based system, defensive medical practices, which, some experts estimate could comprise up to 10% of our $3 trillion healthcare bill, could be exposed and then minimized as the counterproductive force in healthcare delivery that they are.

All this may be possible for the first time through the appropriate and cost effective use of the blizzard of new electronic health information technologies becoming available. A technologically savvy Millennial Generation of both providers and patients working together in a much more real time, collegial, team-based environment provides great hope for achieving all four goals of the Quadruple Aim in the years and decades to come.

James B. Couch, M.D., J.D., FACPE
Princeton, NJ
August, 2014
E-mail: JCouch@jhdgroup.com

FOREWORD

Dr. Couch has captured the ongoing reform of the American healthcare system in a moment of equipoise – a balance he seeks to tip in favor of greater value. He has worked to create positive change in quality and safety over his entire career. His special knowledge of the barriers to achieving better healthcare for individuals and populations at lower cost – the essence of the so-called "Triple Aim" – is captured in his concept of a fourth aim, (the "Quadruple Aim") namely decreased medical liability. This is the focus of his book.

The Triple Aim was made popular by Dr. Donald Berwick during his tenure as the leader of the Institute for Healthcare Improvement, and it remains a term in good currency. It encompasses:

- Improving the patient experience of care (including quality of care and patient satisfaction);
- Improving the health of individuals and populations of patients; and
- Reducing the per capita cost of health care.

Dr. Couch uses a low key informality in this book to be an effective voice for healthcare reform. The reader will discover his passion in the well- crafted pages that offer a "primer" on the state of healthcare. Participants wrestle with the flaws of the fee-for-service system and the unknown, or only partially known, challenges of moving towards value- based care. The "primer" provides the context for thinking about the fourth aim. The constraints of the legal system on grand ideas, fond hopes, and new strategies to improve the healthcare system are very frequently overlooked or underplayed, but this book helps fix that. Dr. Couch argues that we will not see the Triple Aim achieved if we don't also decrease medical liability risk, the fourth goal of the Quadruple Aim.

Dr. Couch addresses a range of critical elements in our intricate healthcare system. He examines both clinical and information technology, financing mechanisms like bundled payments, and the shift towards far more extensive involvement by patients and consumers in their own care and their willingness to pay for that care. He does it well. He does it so well that even the sophisticated reader will find insights in what I'm characterizing as the book's "primer" aspects.

Take for example this single instance: Electronic Health Records (EHRs) increasingly include computerized decision support systems (CDSS) to aid physicians and other providers in tapping an evidence base. CDSS use sophisticated diagnostic and/or therapeutic algorithms to formulate recommendations for clinicians. How might CDSS impact physician liability? Dr. Couch presages the issues that courts will likely raise, questioning whether physicians may be held accountable for knowing as much or more about the evidence base than do these extraordinarily complex systems. But if that is the legal standard to which physicians will be held, why even have computerized decision support diagnostic and therapeutic algorithms? Technological capability and the legal system may be out of synch.

The reader will find scores of other such insights as he or she progresses through this highly readable, extremely current and thoughtful book. In the book's final two chapters, Dr. Couch summarizes his recommendations and presents a vision of how to achieve the Quadruple Aim.

Jeffrey Lerner, Ph.D.
President and CEO; ECRI Institute
5200 Butler Pike
Plymouth Meeting, PA 19462
E-mail: JLerner@ECRI.org

About the Author

Dr. Couch, as a senior physician executive and attorney, has dedicated his career to improving the quality, safety and efficiency of healthcare delivery through the appropriate and judicious use of advanced electronic health information and analytics technologies. Beginning at Penn's Leonard Davis Institute of Health Economics in the 1970s, he focused on how to achieve what is now referred to as the "Triple Aim". Equally as long, as an attorney, he has concentrated on how to simultaneously decrease medical liability risk, the fourth goal of the Quadruple Aim.

Dr. Couch's career spans virtually every component of the $3 trillion healthcare industry. He served as the in house Counsel for Medico-Legal Affairs for the (then) busiest medical defense law firm in Philadelphia. He also was the Chief Medical Quality Officer of a leading academic health system and two "Big 5 Health Insurers". He directed a global disease and health management consulting practice for a "Big 4" professional services firm. He was also the Vice President for Strategic Development, leader of Health IT and Chief Medical Officer of the American Division of the world's largest reinsurance company. Within those roles, he also worked extensively on behalf of pharmaceutical, biotech, life sciences, health IT and analytics companies, venture capital and private equity firms to help accomplish the Quadruple Aim.

He was a charter member of the Health Policy Council of the National Business Group on Health, which supports value based purchasing (VBP) by the Fortune 500. He represented those interests for a Leapfrog Group charter member employer. He helped position New Jersey as a leader of the early rollout of that nationwide VBP initiative. His published work in VBP dates to the 1980s. As the nation's only physician Senior Examiner for the Malcolm

Baldrige National Quality Award from 1992-4, he introduced VBP into that Award's early Healthcare Criteria. He was the first physician in the country trained in Six Sigma and the first to apply it to a health plan in 1992.

Dr. Couch led a double blind, prospective, randomized, controlled clinical trial at a major research university published in a leading academic journal that demonstrated the 707% ROI of an advanced clinical decision making system. President Obama's Director of the White House OMB praised this study and its results in the "Washington Post", as did Former U.S. Speaker of the House, Newt Gingrich, in his breakthrough book: "Saving Lives and Saving Money".

Dr. Couch edited and co-authored three previous major books. His first was "Healthcare Quality Management for the 21st Century" published jointly by the American College of Physician Executives and the American College of Medical Quality in 1991. His second and third books were the "The Physician's Guide to Disease Management" and "The Healthcare Professional's Guide to Disease Management", published, respectively, in 1997 and 1998 by Aspen Publishers, which is now part of Jones & Bartlett Learning.

Dr. Couch has lectured on healthcare quality and policy, risk management, and VBP at Penn's School of Medicine & Wharton Graduate School, Cornell's Medical School, NYU's Stern Business and Wagner School of Public Service, Johns Hopkins, Harvard, Yale and Oxford (Wolfson and Green Colleges). Dr. Couch has a B.A. in Social & Behavioral Sciences from Ohio State University, a J.D. (Doctor of Jurisprudence) from Indiana University Maurer School of Law, and an M.D. from the Perelman School of Medicine at the University of Pennsylvania.

ACKNOWLEDGMENTS

I would like to acknowledge the excellent "Foreword" by my friend and colleague of 30 years, Jeffrey Lerner, Ph.D., President and CEO of the ECRI Institute. The organization he leads, as much as any other, has been dedicated to helping all professionals in the healthcare industry to achieve the Quadruple Aim since its founding almost a half century ago.

I would also like to express my deep appreciation to Nova Science Publishing's leadership. Ms. Nadya Columbus had the vision and courage to grant me the high honor and privilege of being able to weave more than 40 years of my professional and personal "lessons learned" into this book. We believe it to be an unprecedented work designed to help current and future professionals in care delivery and financing, information technology and management, systems engineering, public and population health, law and policymaking to do what's required to create a reformed healthcare system that works best for every stakeholder, especially patients.

Chapter 1

THE EVOLVING POST-REFORM HEALTHCARE LANDSCAPE

GOVERNMENT-FACILITATED MARKET-BASED QUALITY AND COST-BASED COMPETITION

The Patient Protection and Affordable Care Act (hereafter known as the ACA), passed and signed into law on March 23, 2010, is much more than simply a means of extending coverage to approximately 30 of the 50 million Americans without health insurance coverage. Rather, the ACA's real and most long lasting impact has been and will be on the ways that it has catalyzed the transformation of healthcare financing and delivery. There will be much more on these changes and their medical and legal impact in subsequent chapters below.

Presidents and Congresses for a century (since Former President's Teddy Roosevelt's Bull Moose Party platform in 1912) had tried and failed to pass comprehensive healthcare reform. For the ACA to make it through a politically polarized Congress and country between the August Congressional Recess of 2009 (when the Tea Party came into full flower against it) and March of 2010 when it finally passed, it had to appeal to at least three different audiences.

Liberals and Progressives have sought expanded access to healthcare for generations. Americans in the middle class (with moderate means but who were not eligible for government assistance) wanted protections from abusive insurance practices. These practices included denying coverage for pre-existing conditions, medical underwriting resulting in sky high premiums for those who dared to get sick or injured, and the imposing of annual and lifetime limits of coverage with their potential for bankruptcy-producing medical bills even for patients with "good" insurance coverage. Traditional Conservatives (i.e. not including those who have been against anything that President Obama has tried to accomplish legislatively) wanted new models for delivering and financing care to contain costs, while improving quality. They have also wanted medical liability reform.

The most strident criticisms of the ACA have come from the extreme ends of the political spectrum. These have included those who wanted single payer healthcare financing and those who wanted no change whatsoever. Those who wanted no change at all were especially against the individual mandate to purchase coverage (without which insurance companies never would have agreed to curtail their abusive practices of denying coverage discussed in the previous paragraph).

With all its imperfections (including the debacle accompanying the initial rollout of the Healthcare.gov website in October and November of 2013), the ACA has achieved (or likely will eventually achieve) at least to some reasonable extent, the three goals supported by these disparate partisan groups. Probably the biggest criticism of the ACA (at least among these three groups) is that it did not go far enough, although fully satisfying all three of these groups' desires would have been politically impossible.

What emerged from one of the most convoluted sausage-making legislative processes in Congressional history was a very American, hybrid version of healthcare reform, viz. *government-facilitated, market-driven, cost and quality (i.e. value based) competition.* Government's role is to get the insurance industry (and the hospitals, physicians and others who receive payments from it) to begin to compete for the business of employers, the government, and consumers on the basis of the demonstrable value of their care. In the case of insurers, they will be evaluated on the basis of the value of the care and the covered services that their assembled provider networks deliver from the perspectives of those who receive and pay for that care. Individuals are required by the Government to obtain adequate, hopefully affordable, insurance (with the help of government subsidies). This permits insurers to spread the costs deriving from increased access to care of the previously uninsured (and often very sick) and the elimination of coverage-denying or other access-limiting insurance practices.

Libertarians could (and do) see requirements by the government for individuals to acquire and maintain insurance coverage (especially from a relatively limited number of private carriers) as coercive, which, in a sense, is accurate. However, requiring coverage of as many people as possible was necessary to correct what had become an increasingly inefficient, wasteful, unfair (and many would say immoral) private healthcare system. A growing proportion of this private system has been driven by large, profit-driven corporations whose leaders have had to bend to the will of Wall Street investment analysts at least as much as they have to that of their policyholders.

Those in the individual and small business insurance markets have been particularly affected adversely in the absence of the protections of the ACA. Without the purchasing clout of large corporations, unions or the government itself, they have had to face a volatile and unpredictable market. They have had little assurance that they could continue to obtain and retain coverage for themselves, their dependents, or their employees at an affordable price should significant illnesses or injuries befall them or their employees. They also have not had the resources to determine the relative value of whatever coverage they have been able to obtain, much less of the value of the care that they receive from their health plans' contracted networks of hospitals and physicians. Despite extensive state insurance regulations governing the individual and small markets, enforcement has been difficult and inconsistent. It has truly been a "Wild West" for those left to their own devices in this highly fragmented marketplace.

How the health insurance exchanges are intended to begin to remedy this situation is covered more extensively in the next section. How well they will be able to improve the predictability and fairness of this marketplace is a grand experiment to be carried out in 50 state laboratories of change, the results of which will probably not be known until the end of this decade, if then.

State Health Insurance Exchanges: Cost and Quality Transparency Emerges

Despite all the polarizing controversy of the ACA as being a "federal power grab", it will be the individual states (as "laboratories of democracy") where healthcare reform will actually be implemented. The ACA has merely defined the broad parameters for how healthcare services will need to be packaged, financed, delivered, evaluated and rewarded. It will be up to each state to flesh out the unique details as to how all this plays out.

The main vehicle through which healthcare reform will occur is the state health insurance exchange. However, despite its rocky rollout, a full 36 states expect to opt for the federal exchange for the 2015 enrollment period beginning on November 15, 2014. But, every state can still take back control of its own exchange, if desired, and capable of doing so.

The initial debacle accompanying the rollout of the exchanges (especially the federal exchange) is well known. The Dept. of Health and Human Services (DHHS) never imagined that so many states (especially those advocating states' rights in virtually every other endeavor) would opt for the federal exchange model. Consequently, the federal (and some state) exchanges were not able to handle the volume of visits and simultaneous attempts to purchase insurance on the exchanges. That made for a very messy and unproductive first couple of months. Nevertheless, by the end of the first enrollment period, over eight million Americans had become insured through the new exchanges.

There is now more confidence that both the federal and state insurance exchanges can fulfill their most basic function of helping to get Americans covered by health plans meeting requirements for "essential benefits" (at either the Platinum, Gold, Silver, Bronze or Catastrophic insurance levels). Now, their longer-lasting value may be tested. The true worth of the insurance exchanges will be to facilitate cost and quality (i.e. value) based competition among health plans and their contracted hospitals, physicians and other providers.

During the initial rollout, the relative "value" of health plans has been limited to disclosing monthly premium costs. These may be offset by any subsidies due from the federal government depending on the modified adjusted gross income (MAGI) of individuals purchasing coverage for themselves and/or their families. In addition, there has been information about individual or family deductibles, coinsurance and copay requirements. This is an improvement in terms of transparency before the advent of these exchanges. However, this information is not nearly enough for consumers to make truly informed decisions about the plans for which they enlist, much less about the contracted hospitals and physicians of these plans from whom they and their families will receive care.

The demand for transparency will only increase as we pass through this decade. The first time release of Medicare charge and payment data from 880,000 physicians in April, 2014 received front page coverage in newspapers and journals nationwide. That release had been fought by the AMA for 35 years. The release showed that only two percent of physicians were responsible for a whopping $15.1 billion, or 23.4% of the total payments. [1] *Adelson, R and Cohen, S, Sliver of Medicare Doctors Get Big Share of Payout; New York Times; April 9, 2014.*

But that was just the tip of the iceberg in terms of what is to come. On June 1, 2014, the federal government also released two full years of data on inpatient charges for the 100 most frequently billed discharge based on a rate per discharge using the Medicare Severity Diagnosis Related Group (MS-DRG) on more than 3000 U.S. hospitals.

[2] http://www.cms.gov/Research-Statistics-Data-and-Systems/Statistics-Trends-and-Reports/Medicare-Provider-Charge-Data/Inpatient.html

What has changed (and will be changing at an accelerating pace for the rest of this decade and beyond) is the rapidly increasing percentage of healthcare costs which will be borne by patients and their families: See this from a healthcare consumer...

"Greetings Providers! By way of introduction, we've not met before. I am one of the hundreds of millions of people out there who were once referred to as your patients. Going forward, however, it'd be more accurate if you thought of me as a healthcare consumer. This is a business, after all, and you're selling me a product. So, we need to be clear about our new relationship. Let me assure you, now that the rules of healthcare delivery have changed so dramatically, the idea of the healthcare consumer is not a mere buzzword. This is now a matter of my 'skin in the game' and my cold hard cash…Now that I'm the one who will be paying the freight on the first $5000, $7000 or $8000 and higher of my healthcare costs, here's what you can expect from me:

I Want Transparency:

Tell me why I need it and what it's going to cost, up front. Transparency is highest on my list of priorities because without knowing how you do business, when you do business, how much you charge for your business, we can't do business.

I Want it Cheap:

Surveys say that healthcare consumers value 'quality care'. But now that I have to pay more for that quality, I want it cheaper. If your prices are higher, you'd better be able to explain why, but I'll probably still go elsewhere…

I Want it Now:

Don't make me take time off from work to sit in your waiting room for an hour for a harried 15 minute visit with a physician's assistant and a $150 bill. Drug stores are open 24/7. Banks are open later. Even airlines are more consumer-friendly than providers…I don't see my demands as unreasonable. I am merely asking the healthcare sector—a $2.8 trillion industry that consumes nearly 20% of the gross domestic product—to be as accountable and transparent with its products as any other retail industry…

So, I hope we are clear on what you can expect from our new relationship in the coming years…If you thought it was rough haggling with insurance companies, wait 'til you get a load of me."

[3] http://www.healthleadersmedia.com/content/COM-299794/A-Letter-to-Healthcare-Providers-from-a-Consumer

Transparency in healthcare pricing and outcomes to promote a more value based healthcare financing system under the ACA will also have profound effects on the potential for and actuality of medical liability. According to a recently published study by Patient Safety America using the evidence based "Global Trigger Tool", medical errors may kill over 400,000 hospitalized patients every year. In addition, the incidence of serious (vs. lethal) harm resulting from medical errors may be 10 to 20 times greater.

[4] http://www.ncbi.nlm.nih.gov/pubmed/23860193

This much higher than previously issued estimate of hospital patient deaths due to medical errors (now the third leading cause of death in America), coupled with the much higher percentage of medical bills paid by consumers could result in significantly increased medical liability. This means the "average" American hospital is killing about 100 patients per year due to medical errors, and causing serious harm from errors in as many as 2000 patients per year or to about a half dozen each and every day!

As made clear in the extensive diatribe by the new healthcare consumer quoted above, patients (in all clinical settings) will expect much more from their healthcare providers now that they will have a great deal more "skin in the game". They will demand the transparency required for them to make informed choices about the providers (hospitals, physicians, et. al.) from whom they receive care. They will want to know if their providers who are contracted with their health plans are working in hospitals that are one or more standard deviations above or below the mean for lethal and serious medical errors. If possible, they would like this information at the physician level (assuming that could be done with any degree of statistical significance). Also, if possible and statistically meaningful, they would like this medical error rate information (resulting in either lethal or serious harm) to be condition-specific (e.g. for heart attacks, heart failure, pneumonias, strokes, surgical procedure, etc.).

The new healthcare consumer may be lucky enough to find within a health plan contracted hospitals and physicians who rank one, two or even three standard deviations better than the mean for medical error incidence and severity of illness adjusted, condition-specific clinical outcomes. However, he or she is still going to want at least that same level of transparency about likely out of pocket diagnostic and treatment costs. The protective cocoon of relative financial immunity from healthcare costs continues to melt away. The new healthcare consumer will demand (for really the first time) the same degree of value demonstration and accountability from the healthcare industry and medical profession as he or she has expected from all other retail establishments. The name of the game in healthcare will increasingly be accountability for results and demonstration of value. That is the central goal of the new delivery and financing vehicles rapidly emerging from the ACA and out of economic necessity, as covered in the next section.

Accountable Care Organizations to Become the Healthcare Delivery Norm

What in the ACA has received much less publicity (at least in the popular press) than the ill-fated healthcare.gov rollout has been its strong support of alternative healthcare delivery models, especially Accountable Care Organizations (hereafter ACOs). At the present time, between those sponsored (or financed) by the public and private sectors, there are over 650 ACOs up and going (split about 60/40 between public and private sectors, respectively). Those ACOs that have received the most publicity (and have had the most transparency regarding how they need to operate and produce to be clinically and financially successful) have been those sponsored by the Centers for Medicare and Medicaid Services (hereafter CMS). These have been those announced (as having gained their status as the result of a competitive bidding process) as part of the CMS Medicare Shared Savings Program (hereafter CMS MSSP). There have also been leading edge Pioneer ACOs and those that have been part of Beacon Communities and others serving as demonstration projects for the Centers for Medicare and Medicaid Innovation (CMMI).

Getting into a detailed comparative analysis of ACOs (whether publicly or privately financed by insurers, employers or others) is beyond the scope of this book. However, what is most important about all of them can be summarized as follows:

- They represent a coming together of care facilities (acute, sub-acute and chronic) and the physicians and other caregivers who serve in them;

- They are chartered to take care of the health needs of distinct populations of patients covered financially by a public or private sector as sponsor (e.g. Medicare or Medicaid patients, insured patients in health plans, those in a geographic area served by hospitals/health systems or medical groups, or perhaps even employees of large companies or unions);
- They either initially, or (in most cases, eventually) are expected to assume some (or even all) financial risk for the costs of diagnosing and treating these patient populations for specific, contractually defined time periods;
- They are also expected to meet or exceed specific quality of care standards (both by adhering to best evidence based practices and/or achieving specified clinical outcomes of their patients). These may either be absolute requirements (or relatively weighted through the production of quality scores based on the actual outcomes of patients, and/or the degree of improvements noted from previous baseline periods of measured performance); and
- They reward provider participants in these ACOs (especially those also taking on downside financial risks) commensurate with their ability to demonstrate their quality (including performance improvement as defined above). They are also evaluated and rewarded based on their relative cost effectiveness in managing the needs of their patients for whose health needs and overall costs of care they are accountable to their sponsors and their beneficiaries for contractually designated time periods.

The liability implications arising from medical errors identified as causing harm to patients receiving care from providers (of all types) participating in ACOs having these characteristics are too numerous to mention here. They will be covered in more detail in subsequent chapters.

Suffice it to say, however, that by its very name *(Accountable* Care Organization), it stands to reason that ACOs will be held to a different (presumably higher) standard should suboptimal care by providers participating in them be proven to be the direct and proximate cause of compensable injury to patients. However, what will that new standard of care be? Will it be determined by whatever quality requirements are set in the ACO agreement that need to be met to qualify for sharing in the savings that may accrue after the final accounting of the costs for treating a particular population in the specified time period?

What if the alleged injury occurred before the ACO (or the providers participating in it) had just implemented a quality improvement program to address possible safety issues with a specific diagnostic or therapeutic procedure or other treatment? The law usually seeks to exclude from evidence the fact of the implementation of safety measures to address situations which may have resulted in harm. Otherwise, the whole purpose of accountable care to continuously improve the quality, safety and efficiency of care through ongoing evaluation and implementation of enhancements would be severely undermined. ACO participants would fear that such interventions could be evidence that unsafe conditions were responsible for the avoidable harm that may have become the subject of litigation.

VALUE BASED PURCHASING & BUNDLED PAYMENTS TO BECOME THE FINANCING NORM

Fee for service, which compensates physicians for each service that they deliver, is the most common payment model for healthcare in the United States. Currently, about 79% of workers (and 73% of all state and local government workers), who are enrolled in health insurance are in fee for service plans.

[5] http://www.bls.gov/ncs/ebs

Most policymakers see fee for service as playing a major role in driving up healthcare spending. The model provides a financial incentive for providers to maximize the number and cost of services they deliver. At the same time, it does not reward superior care, better outcomes, or increased efficiency.

The State Health Care Cost Containment Commission (co-chaired by two former Governors and a former Republican HHS Secretary) concluded in a January, 2014 report from the Miller Center at the University of Virginia (led by a Former Governor of Virginia) that the fee for service payment system was a major cause of per capita healthcare costs in the U.S. being more than 150% higher than (any of) those in the rest of the major industrialized nations worldwide. With the full implementation of the ACA and a strengthening economy, this gap was only expected to widen over the course of the rest of this decade, resulting in per capita costs of $14,103 by 2021, consuming 19.6% of the GDP.

[6] *Leavitt, M., Ritter, B, Cracking the Code on Healthcare Costs: A Report by the State Health Care Cost Containment Commission; p. 36; University of Virginia Miller Center; Charlottesville, VA (2014)*

The ACA anticipated the need to move away from the fee for service system by accelerating trends toward bundled payments, capitation and other forms of value based compensation (sometimes known as, although not entirely accurately or sufficiently, as "pay for performance"). The inpatient value based purchasing payment system for the reimbursement of inpatient services for Medicare patients has been in place in the nation's approximately 5000 nonfederal hospitals since October, 2012. The value based payment modifier (VPM) system for the reimbursement of physician services to Medicare patients will continue to be phased in during 2015 with the addition of efficiency measures requiring that the cost of delivering care be factored into the complex VPM formula.

In addition, the Medicare reimbursement penalty for being a "readmissions outlier" went from 1 to 2% of payments in Federal Fiscal Year (FFY) 2014 and is scheduled to increase to 3% in FFY 2015. Plus, there continue to be penalties for having "too many" hospital acquired conditions (HAC) and healthcare associated infections (HAI). Additionally, there may be (TBD) financial penalties for either not having started to "meaningfully use" electronic health records by 2015, or not electronically prescribing by then.

The individual percentage decreases to Medicare reimbursements for these (and other) deficiencies is still relatively small (usually in the one to three percent range). However, in the aggregate, these penalties begin to approach (or even exceed) the 10% of total reimbursement figure which behavioral economists believe is required to significantly alter clinical decision making. What may also happen, in the interim, is how the legal system may regard the failure to earn complete reimbursement as a result of not having delivered superior value care (e.g. high readmission, HAC and/or HAI rates, as well as failure to meaningfully use EHRs and/or to prescribe electronically). Another example of value based purchasing (VBP) to achieve certain quality and cost effectiveness goals follows.

The federal government in 2013 began sponsoring approximately 500 bundled payment arrangements with hospitals, health systems and physician groups around the country. Private payers have sponsored these arrangements for some years also (including health systems like Geisinger—see more on that below). The defining principle of all bundled payment arrangements is that the hospitals, health systems (including all its non-acute facility components) and/or physicians are paid a pre-set sum of money for providing the diagnostic and treatment needs of a specific population of patients (including particular invasive procedures when indicated) for a given time period, or illness episode.

To receive complete payment, however, these providers also must achieve agreed upon quality (process and outcomes of care) and cost containment goals. Bundled payments may cover the costs of treatment of specific population groups and subgroups within the inpatient setting. However, more likely, the bundled payments cover the costs across the care continuum from inpatient to sub-acute, to outpatient rehabilitation, to physician clinic visits for a specific time period (or episode of illness). Bundling of payments to physicians and to facilities may also occur to cover the costs of the preparation for, execution of, and recovery from various types of invasive procedures such as coronary artery bypass grafts, total knee or hip replacements, and many other types of therapeutic interventions.

From a medico-legal perspective, bundled payments may begin to approximate a "product of care", much more closely than was possible under the open-ended fee for service system. Geisinger Health Systems (GHS) for some time now has been providing what could be described as a "warranty" for the treatment of its coronary patients. GHS accepts a fixed (with some adjustments) payment for the treatment of its heart patients over a 90 day period from the initial intake at the Emergency Room, through time in the Coronary Care Unit, to Step-Down, to a regular hospital bed, to cardiac rehabilitation, to outpatient clinic with cardiologists, back to the primary care physician. This is part of its "ProvenCare" program.

[7] http:// www.geisinger.org/provencare/

There may be extenuating pre-treatment severity of illness circumstances to adjust payments upwards or downwards. Nevertheless, there also is at least an implied warranty that optimal care (according to the best evidence based medical standards) must be delivered (in the absence of justifiable exceptions) in order to receive the full, prospectively agreed upon reimbursement for the treatment of such patients in this program. If this type of arrangement could be interpreted as rising to the level of an implied warranty for care results, or at least of the process to achieve those results, this could raise a whole new spectrum (and specter) of medical liability potential.

A more thorough discussion of the information technologies necessary for driving healthcare delivery and financing transformation follows below in Chapter 2.

Chapter 2

INFORMATION TECHNOLOGIES DRIVING HEALTHCARE DELIVERY AND FINANCING TRANSFORMATION

ELECTRONIC HEALTH RECORDS: THEIR EVOLUTION AND POTENTIAL LIABILITY IMPLICATIONS

Electronic Health Records (hereafter EHRs) have been highly touted as indispensable to facilitate healthcare reform. The transformative movements of accountable care and value based purchasing (VBP) will need to be supported by the widespread implementation and appropriate use of interoperable EHRs.

The history of electronic health records may be traced back to the work of pioneers such as Drs. William Stead (from Vanderbilt) and Octo Barnett (from Harvard), among others, in the 1960s. For most hospitals (and especially physicians), EHRs remained mostly in a theoretical world inhabited by IT geeks until at least the 1980s. At about that time, some of the well-known integrated health systems (such as Kaiser, Intermountain, and Geisinger, among a few others) began to develop and implement early versions of EHRs. Even this author had some early exposure to EHRs in the middle 1980s as the Chief Medical Quality Officer of an academic medical center in Philadelphia. That institution became an early adopter of the "Technicon System". That system employed a "Magic Wand" to facilitate electronic ordering by physicians.

These prototypical systems began to be replaced by EHRs by General Electric, Cerner, Siemens, and McKesson, among others, in the 1990s. However, to a great extent, during this time (and even until fairly recently), these systems also were not terribly user-friendly, or functionally effective, in demonstrably improving the quality, safety and efficiency (i.e. "value") of healthcare delivery.

This author worked extensively with leading technology and medical professionals from five such EHR firms (eClinical Works, McKesson, NextGen, MiSys and Eclipsys—the latter two both now part of Allscripts) during 2008. The purpose of this collaboration was to determine the extent to which these systems (when properly implemented and used by physicians and other caregivers) could minimize the incidence of the primary causes of medical liability. These causes had been determined by an extensive analysis of medical malpractice claims handled by the Princeton Insurance Company using an analytic tool from the Harvard Risk Management Foundation.

[8] *Electronic Health Records Patient Safety and Risk Management Guide; Princeton Insurance Company; Princeton, NJ (2008).*

http://www.pinsco.com/downloads/EMRUsersGuide_final.pdf

Deriving from this comprehensive analysis of claims filed over a six year period, the four most prevalent reasons for liability were identified as the following:

- Communication Gaps (between provider and patient or between providers);
- Medical Record "Defects" (either as to the mechanics or the sufficiency of medical recordkeeping);
- Ineffective Office Practices and Clinical Systems (including practice management alert systems to track and follow up with patients, as well as to provide screening and preventive health reminders); and
- Problems with Clinical Judgment and Unexpectedly Bad Clinical Outcomes (deriving from suboptimal diagnostic and therapeutic process and decision making)

All the vendors (listed above) brought their top medical, technology and marketing professionals into Princeton Insurance to respond to a detailed set of approximately 50 questions. These questions covered how their systems could be (and are) used by physicians and other providers to minimize the incidence of these demonstrated causes of medical liability. They were able to do this not only by responding to the scripted questions, but also by showing how their systems could actually do this through live demonstrations. They could augment their "business cases" then by submitting (as they did) hundreds of additional actual screen shots from their EHR systems. These were to demonstrate how, *used properly*, their systems could further decrease these causes of medical liability.

This author, with leading risk management executives from Princeton Insurance, then interviewed physician, practice manager and nurse users to determine whether the claims by the EHR executives held up in actual practice. We visited with the providers at their practices who had implemented and used these systems for as short a time period as six months to more than 10 years. We saw the systems in practice, including their use during actual patient examinations. We received their unvarnished opinions concerning whether they could (and were) being used to minimize the documented causes of medical liability.

Finally, we interviewed key medical liability defense attorneys who were representing Princeton Insurance policyholders with scripted questions also concerning their own experience in defending physicians, hospitals and other providers in which the use, nonuse, misuse or abuse of EHRs was at issue (among other matters) in their cases. The questions we posed to this third group correlated closely with those we asked of both the EHR vendors and the provider users of their systems to maintain as much consistency as possible across all interviewees.

From all this information, Princeton Insurance was able to compile an unprecedented, comprehensive patient safety and risk management guide (see Reference #8, above) for all Princeton-insured hospitals and physicians throughout New Jersey. This guide covered how to implement (and even more importantly how to use and not to misuse or abuse) EHRs (of all types) to minimize the incidence of the risks determined to result in medical liability. This Princeton Insurance study was cited in a 2013 published "Editors' Correspondence" in "*JAMA Internal Medicine*" as providing the blueprint on how to use EHRs to achieve the "Quadruple Aim" in healthcare (viz. to improve its quality, patient outcomes, and cost effectiveness, while decreasing risks of liability).

[9] *Couch, J.B., How to Use Electronic Health Records to Achieve the Quadruple Aim; JAMA Internal Medicine; 173(3):250 (February, 2013).*

Recommendations deriving from this study for using EHRs to minimize the demonstrated risks leading to medical liability will be discussed later in Chapter 5. What follows, immediately below, is an introduction of some of the more advanced types of electronic health information technologies and how they are (and will be) used in the years and decades ahead to address the goals of the Quadruple Aim.

Computerized Physician Order Entry (CPOE) and Patient Management

Computerized physician order entry (hereafter CPOE) has been around since at least the 1980s. As stated earlier, when this author was the Chief Medical Quality Officer at an academic medical center in Philadelphia, a type of CPOE was introduced there as the technology of the future (see the previous discussion of the Technicon system above). The whole notion behind CPOE was that having physicians enter their orders through a computer system (rather than by their often illegible handwriting) would minimize medical errors and greatly improve efficiency in nurses' receipt and implementation of those orders.

The Leapfrog Group (LFG) was founded by Fortune 500 CEOs comprising the membership of the Business Roundtable in 2000 to foster value based purchasing among the nation's largest employers. The LFG made having functional and effective CPOE as one of its first three (and probably most controversial) requirements for hospitals and health systems. Hospitals for the past decade have been evaluated by the LFG concerning how well they have implemented and are using CPOE (as well as other quality improvement practices and methodologies to ensure safe and effective healthcare delivery).

What proved controversial about the CPOE requirement was multifaceted in nature. First, CPOE systems were quite expensive. Second, at least the earlier versions of them were rather cumbersome to use. Third, they were rather clunky in design (and often required toggling between many screens to enter even simple orders). Consequently, they may have actually *increased* the opportunities and actual incidences of errors (which, were then propagated at the "speed of light"). For more on how the use of CPOE could actually *increase* the opportunities for medication mistakes, refer to the important study by Dr. Ross Koppel and his team at the University of Pennsylvania.

[10] *Koppel R, Metlay JP, Cohen A, Abaluck B, Localio AR, Kimmel SE, Strom BL: Role of computerized physician order entry systems in facilitating medication errors. J Am Med Assoc 2005, 293:1197-1203.*

It is well known among Six Sigma quality assessment and improvement experts that the greater the opportunities for error in any process, the greater the number of errors that actually occur. This holds true even when the quality and effectiveness of the execution of the individual steps of a process remain the same. So, the mere introduction of CPOE, which may disrupt previously well-traveled clinical process workflows, may (for that reason alone) result in the production of more (and/or new and different types of) errors. This increased process complexity could provide at least one of the explanations for the facilitation of new types of medical errors by the introduction of CPOE as found in the Koppel study cited above.

This well-established principle of Six Sigma also explains, in a much larger sense, why our entire $3 trillion healthcare system is so error prone. The still predominant fee for service system (coupled with defensive medicine practices) results in strong financial and medico-legal risk management incentives, respectively, to do everything possible to rule in or rule out specific diagnoses. This volume-driven reimbursement system and fear of litigation also provide incentives to treat patients aggressively (sometimes regardless of their actual needs or desires) when discretion would be the better part of valor. Physicians were taught in medical school (and beyond) to consider every *possible* diagnosis and (often invasive and even risky) tests and procedures to rule in or rule out as many conditions as possible, including those that may have been quite unlikely as the root causes of patients' chief complaints.

This approach was considered to be essential to the teaching and learning process of becoming a physician. Fortunately, some (and now an increasing percentage of) physicians did not buy into this. They focused more on the patient's and his/her families' financial and social (as well as) medical needs. They limited the use of invasive and costly diagnostic and therapeutic tests and procedures to those patients where the results from such interventions *more likely than not* (as opposed to *possibly*) would make a positive difference in their medical management, outcomes, and quality of life. So long as fee for service reigned supreme, such progressive-minded physicians were hurt financially. They may even have been perceived as placing themselves, their partner physicians and institutions at increased medico-legal risk. However, as covered in more detail below, taking this more rational approach, should not only improve the value of care to patients, but also decrease medical liability risk to physicians.

In the meantime, however, electronic health information technologies may be used to achieve the opposite effect. There has recently been an increasing number of reports that have pointed out that the use of electronic health information technologies may actually result in greater opportunities for overutilization (whether intentional or unintentional), even fraud.

[11] *Abelson, R, et al., Medicare Bills Rise as Records Become Electronic; New York Times; Sept. 21, 2012.*

Using these technologies in this way would completely subvert their purpose to improve the demonstrable quality, safety, effectiveness and efficiency (i.e. the value) of healthcare delivery. They may be used to take advantage of the pay for volume reimbursement system (as it still continues to predominate) rather than to use these systems to promote (or at least respond effectively to) one that rewards demonstrable value.

Choosing this less noble approach will almost surely result in increased, rather than decreased medico-legal liability. Plaintiffs' attorneys and their experts who can demonstrate not only negligence when using these advanced health information technologies, but also tainted motivations to use them to make more money (whether legally or illegally) will have a much easier time making their case to the judge or jury. In such cases, punitive damages may well be in order, in addition to large recoveries for compensable injuries. Fortunately, it does not appear at the present time that the use of EHRs to overutilize services (honestly or fraudulently) is a significant problem. However, until value based purchasing becomes the predominant reimbursement methodology throughout the country, at least the incentive for the abuse of these electronic health information technologies to achieve unwarranted financial gain will remain present.

PREDICTIVE MODELING SYSTEMS AND THE ROLE OF "BIG DATA"

Various precursors to today's predictive modeling systems have been in use by the insurance industry for years, even decades, in some cases. Their fundamental purpose has been to be able to predict the likely future costs that a specific covered population will incur in a given time period. This permits actuaries to "rate" that population mathematically and underwriters then to set premium levels for policyholders (or those paying premiums on their behalf such as employers in the case of health insurance). The goal of rating and underwriting is so that the actual costs produced are less than the aggregate premiums collected. The actual medical costs which carriers are liable to pay divided by the aggregate dollars of premiums collected to cover that same time period is known as the "medical loss ratio" (or MLR).

The MLR is a very important ratio for health insurance companies, especially those that are investor-owned. They need to meet their earnings per share or EPS projections every quarter. Investment analysts use the MLR as a key measure to recommend continued investment in stockholder-owned health insurance companies (like Aetna, Cigna, Humana, WellPoint, United, et. al.).

However, after the ACA, these companies can no longer do this by skimping on systems and infrastructure to improve the quality and value of their offerings. They must be able to demonstrate that 80% to 85% of their premium dollars every year are dedicated to helping to finance the delivery of healthcare and improving its quality and value. Otherwise, they will be liable for rebating premiums to their policyholders to the extent that they don't achieve these milestones. So, predictive modeling systems have taken on an even greater importance for health insurance companies after passage of the ACA.

It has only been in the past few years, however, that predictive modeling systems began to be of interest to providers (especially integrated healthcare delivery systems). As providers enter into accountable care organizations (whether sponsored by payers or by themselves), they increasingly will need to take on and understand how to predict and manage medical risk if they are to be financially successful. Consequently, they will need to become equally familiar with their capabilities to optimize the use of sophisticated predictive modeling systems.

The type of predictive modeling systems which providers involved in accountable care organizations (ACOs), patient-centered medical homes (PCMH), bundled payment arrangements and other value based compensation models will likely use will be somewhat different from those which health insurance companies have been using for years and decades. Insurers have needed to be concerned about what the projected likely costs were going to be to cover a specific patient population with insurance. This insurance coverage was not only rated and underwritten to ensure profitability as explained above. It also may have had restricted lists of health benefits for subscribers, narrow physician and hospital networks with huge out of network payment requirements for patients, increasing out of pocket copayment, coinsurance, deductible stipulations, and other policy limitations. These may have even included (at least prior to the ACA's prohibitions of these) pre-existing illness exclusions and annual and lifetime care cost reimbursement limits.

All in all, at least prior to the ACA, investor-owned health insurance companies enjoyed a tremendous amount of flexibility (and ultimate clout against their policyholders). They could hold the line on MLR and continue to be able to meet their quarterly EPS projections necessary to support their increasingly lofty share prices and top executives' compensation packages. These packages even included huge golden parachutes for top executives sent packing, when earnings didn't meet expectations.

Providers taking on financial risk in the context of one or more of the previously mentioned value based compensation models must focus not only on managing financial, but also, *clinical* risk. Contractual provisions in ACOs may include language that the providers participating in them must be able to demonstrate at least a 95% adherence rate to best evidence based medical practices. These requirements would apply especially for the highest cost, highest prevalence and highest practice variability conditions within the patient populations for whom these ACOs may be held both financially *and clinically* accountable.

To share in savings above periodically allocated amounts of funds to support the care of patient populations covered by these new payment models, participating providers need to demonstrate the quality of their care. It will be especially important for them to be able to do this for patients with multiple chronic conditions and those undergoing specific invasive procedures. Providers will need to be able to demonstrate that their patients' outcomes have also improved. Metrics will include a whole range of "before" and "after" indicators of health status, quality of life and functional capacity.

So, predictive modeling systems of the future (i.e. in the next three to five years) will need to be highly accurate at projecting the likely future medical costs of particular covered populations. However, they must also be able to predict the clinical outcomes of patients, individually and collectively. To do this, they will need to be able to access and analyze accurately so-called "Big Data" concerning the mix and comparative severity of illness load of specific populations at the beginning of a covered time period. By analyzing this data, users of these systems will need to be able to evaluate what should be the likely extent of improvement in clinical outcomes (including quality of life and various functional indicators) for specific covered populations. They will then need to be able to compare to these projections accurately and fairly the actual extent of the improvement in the clinical outcomes of the patients of those providers. Finally, users of these (and other) such systems will also need to have documented (electronically) their 95% or better adherence to best evidence based medical practices for the treatment of patients having the highest cost, prevalence and practice variability in results.

Being able to produce these (and other) types of quality and financial reports will be required of new risk-based payment and delivery organizations to be clinically and financially successful. Imagine, however, for a moment, the extent of the potential medical legal accountabilities that may derive from these new found capabilities in predictive modeling systems. These will be discussed in more detail in Chapter 6.

POPULATION HEALTH AND PERSONALIZED MEDICINE ANALYTICS SYSTEMS

Medical practice (and litigation arising from it) has focused primarily on individual patients for centuries. Was the individual patient evaluated properly and completely? Were the necessary and appropriate diagnostic interventions employed? Did the physician obtain all necessary tests, and interpret every bit of information collected on the patient accurately to arrive at the most likely diagnosis in a timely manner? Did the patient receive the most effective care interventions when they had the greatest opportunity for improving their health?

As discussed earlier, the fee for service payment system, which has continued to predominate since World War II, has emphasized this focus on the individual both in medical practice and in litigation. However, the slow but sure movement away from fees for the volume of services to fees for the value of those services is shifting the focus now towards population health management. Providers must now begin to function like payers. They must assume, understand, analyze, and manage the medical risk of defined populations. They have to think in terms of what the entire group of patients for whose clinical and financial results they will be held accountable will need to improve their collective health status in measurable, demonstrable ways. Failure to do so will result in their not achieving the clinical quality improvement and financial cost effectiveness goals required for them to share rewards in risk bearing initiatives.

In some ways flowing against this trend toward a focus on optimizing the health of populations (vs. each individual patient) is the introduction of the field of genomics into medical management. The mapping of the human genome has ushered in the era of "personalized medicine". Soon, many (if not most) patients may have their entire genomic fingerprints on machine readable cards.

Doing this may help physicians to prescribe only those therapies which have the greatest likelihood of helping individual patients manage (if not eliminate) their specific medical conditions, while minimizing any collateral damage to their healthy tissues and organs. Records of these transactions (including the evidence of what therapies work best for what types of patients with certain conditions and particular genetic footprints) will be uploaded into "Big Databases".

Encrypted and password-protected personal medical information will be accessed not only for those patients, but others with comparable conditions, illness severities, and genetic profiles.

Given this somewhat schizoid focus for treating more cost effectively both populations *and* individual patients, the most sophisticated analytics systems must be well equipped to help providers to accommodate to both emerging emphases. However, the prime mover in medical litigation (at least for the foreseeable future) is still likely to be the individual patient/plaintiff.

On the other hand, as physicians and other providers adapt to a more population-based approach, there may well be an increasing number of class actions by plaintiffs. There may be cases in which entire groups or subgroups of patients with particular conditions allege that they have not been treated optimally according to the latest, best evidence based medical practices. Such class actions could be launched by patients with comparable genetic footprints whose care for specific conditions did not include therapies specifically designed to achieve optimal outcomes.

All of the above discussions still focus primarily on the relationship between physicians and patients. These do not even begin to explore the relationship between patients and their families with the multitude of (new and different) entities that will be assisting physicians in the care of patients in the future. A non-exhaustive list of these may include:

- The manufacturers of the individual and population health analytics tools intended to facilitate their clinical decision making;
- The compilers (for lack of a better term) of genomic and proteomic profile information onto machine readable cards; and
- The producers of personalized medicine therapies (including genetic engineering and comparable treatments designed for managing the conditions of patients with similar genomic and proteomic profiles).

Many of these producers of products may find themselves subject to the laws of product liability. Theories of liability may include, in some cases, implied warranties of fitness, and, even strict product liability (thereby relieving the plaintiff of even having to prove negligence in order to recover damages).

DECISION SUPPORT SYSTEMS: WATSON & OTHER ARTIFICIAL INTELLIGENCE SYSTEMS

Millions got their first introduction to the IBM Watson Supercomputer on a special edition of the longstanding game show, "Jeopardy". Considered the brainiest of that genre of game shows, Watson more than tripled the winnings of those who had previously been the top two all-time Jeopardy grand champions without even breaking a sweat. Watson sifted through 66 million pages of data per second and has only gotten faster and smarter since.

[12] *Hobson, K., Meet Dr. Watson: The IBM Whiz Kid's Work on Cancer is an Early Step in Tapping Big Data; U.S. News & World Report Best Hospitals 2014 Edition; pp. 28-30 (2013).*

Watson is equipped with a 15 terabyte databank, and massively parallel 2,880 processor cores. This makes it incredibly useful to analyze huge datasets which, heretofore, have gone unexamined. Watson's most highly publicized (and potentially valuable) post-Jeopardy gigs have been in healthcare, most notably, the University of Maryland's School of Medicine, Memorial Sloan-Kettering Cancer Center, the Cleveland Clinic Lerner School of Medicine, Columbia University College of Physicians and Surgeons, and WellPoint (among others).

"What makes Watson unique is its ability to absorb text that isn't in a standardized format, such as a doctor's case notes, and pull out the most relevant ideas. And it learns from experience, says Marty Kohn, IBM's chief medical scientist. The more cases Watson sees, and the more interaction it has with users who point out additional sources, Watson should consider, the better it gets. Watson's foray into oncology (at Memorial Sloan Kettering) is only the first baby step toward applying "big data" to thorny medical problems".

[12] *Hobson, K., USN&WR 2014 Best Hospitals at 29*

"By one estimate, health information—electronic health records, insurance claims, images such as CT scans, vital signs of people being remotely monitored by hospitals or smartphones, and gene sequencing results—will grow to the equivalent of about 500 billion four-drawer file cabinets by 2020, from a mere 10 billion in 2011. High-powered computers and new algorithms have the potential to allow physicians and researchers to combine and decipher all that information and see what connections pop. Ideally, medicine would then be able to better track and predict the spread of disease, and diagnose, treat and prevent it, all while improving safety and lowering costs".

[12] *Hobson, K, USN& WR 2014 Best Hospitals at 29*

Seeing the potential for Watson (especially in helping to transform the $3 trillion healthcare industry), IBM has recently invested $1 billion to create a whole division focused on optimizing Watson's value to IBM's customers and itself. In addition, IBM has a plan to "democratize" Watson, while significantly increasing its ultimate computing power, by making its computational capabilities available through the internet (to which it was prohibited to connect during its "Jeopardy" match). Many of its capabilities may soon be commonplace on smartphones. There may soon be a "Wiki-Watson" that could bring together the whole world's medical literature and clinical expertise.

[13] *Gelenter, D., Coming Next: A Supercomputer Saves Your Life; Wall Street Journal, Op-Ed (February, 2011)*

While Dr. Watson is certainly the most high profile of the recent technologies being adapted for use to improve clinical decision making by physicians (and, soon by patients, also), it is certainly not the only one. The clinical decision support system (hereafter CDSS), Isabel, for example, has been gaining increasing support (and even endorsements from major healthcare organizations such as the American Medical Association) during the past few years.

[14] http://www.isabelhealthcare.com

Named after a London investment banker's three year old daughter, who nearly died from a missed diagnosis at a leading U.K. National Health Service (NHS) hospital, her father gave up his profession as an investment banker and formed the company bearing his daughter's name. Even in its early years, Isabel proved to be quite accurate, suggesting the final diagnosis in 95 to 98% of real cases in multi-center clinical studies

[15] *Isabel: A Web-Based Differential Diagnostic Aid for Pediatrics—Results from an Initial Performance Evaluation. Archives of Disease of Childhood; May, 2003.*

It has since become even more widespread in its use as its utility has become better known and accepted. Jason Maude, company co-founder (and the father of Isabel Maude) at the end of 2012 announced the availability of a consumer-friendly version (called "Symptom Checker") of Isabel's core differential diagnostic system. This was intended to improve the interactions between physicians and patients, who have often brought reams of medical information to their appointments, much of which had never been verified. It also furthers the whole "democratization" movement in healthcare. He said the consumer symptom checker allows patients to put together their own differentials, print out the results and compare their findings with the doctor's. "I hope this may be a radical change," Maude said.

[16] http://www.informationweek.com/healthcare/patient-tools/Isabel-opens-online-diagnostic-system-to-consumer/d/d-id/1107794?

MOBILE HEALTH TECHNOLOGIES

There may well be no more democratizing force in healthcare in the years and decades ahead than mobile health (or mhealth). Card-carrying members of the Millennial Generation--those 80 million Americans born between 1980 and 2000--have been using many of these technologies almost since the cradle. They will use these technologies to even the playing field (if not tilt it in their favor) when dealing with the healthcare system (whether for their own care or for that of their young children and/or aging Baby Boomer parents).

For centuries, patients' contact with the healthcare system was primarily defined by visits to physicians or hospitals. Patients, for the most part, did not have the ready knowledge or wherewithal to challenge, or even seriously question, what their physicians recommended or what those treating them in hospitals did for them. Even if these recommendations were sound, other than feeling better (eventually), which may have occurred even in the absence of any intervention, patients had no way of knowing whether their trips to their physicians (or even to hospitals) were really worthwhile.

Of course, with third party payers still picking up the significant majority of the costs, other than the time spent and aggravation caused, patients didn't seem to care about (or even want to know) the relative effectiveness of the care that they received. Besides, during the 99.9% of time that they were not in direct contact with their physicians or other providers, unless they continued to feel bad and/or were incapacitated from their jobs or other pursuits, the results of their care was not a top of mind concern for them. However, there are three major forces now driving healthcare which have been (and certainly will be) changing (if not completely inverting) the power structure between patients and their physicians. *These are: Economics, Technology and Data.*

As more and more of the cost burden falls on patients and their families, they will increasingly care about the effectiveness of the care that they receive. Is the care returning them to their previous state of health, or at least to the point that they can continue to function in their roles as workers, spouses, parents, friends, etc.? The more that patients have to invest financially (not to mention of their time and trouble) to restoring their health, the greater the return on that investment they will expect. They will become not just patients, but customers with choices, who have a right to expect results and a hassle-free process to achieving those results for the money that they spend. That represents the new (and rapidly growing) impact of basic value-driven economics on the healthcare industry.

However, patients and their families will need to be able to access and use real time information to understand how their health status is improving (or not) during that 99.9% of their lives, when, most of them are not directly engaged in the healthcare system. Otherwise, they will not be in a position to assess the return on their investment in health interventions. That's where all the new types of technologies to monitor, measure, track, and trend a whole host of health status indicators and other relevant information in real time enter the picture. Consider the following from Dr. Eric Topol, renowned cardiologist and medical futurist:

"For the first time, we can digitize humans. We can remotely and continuously monitor each heartbeat, moment-to-moment blood pressure readings, the rate and depth of breathing, body temperature, oxygen concentration in the blood, glucose, brain waves, activity, mood—all the things that makes us tick. We can image any part of the body and do a three-dimensional reconstruction, eventually leading to the capability of printing an organ. Or, we can use a miniature, handheld, high-resolution imaging device that rapidly captures critical information anywhere, such as the scene of a motor vehicle accident or a person's home in response to a call of distress. We can determine all 6 billion letters ('life codes') of a person's genome sequence. And all of this information about an individual can be assembled from wireless biosensors, genome sequencing or imaging to be readily available, integrated with all the traditional medical data and constantly updated. We now have the technology to digitize a human being in the highest definition, in granular detail, and in ways that most people thought would not be possible."

[17] *Topol, E, How Technology is Transforming Health Care—Digital Devices are Empowering the Patient and Changing the Face of Healthcare; Excerpted from Eric Topol, "The Creative Destruction of Medicine"; Basic Books (2012) as reproduced in U.S News & World Report; 2014 Best Hospitals Edition; pp. 3-7 (2013).*

The profound impact that economics, technology and data will have on achieving the quadruple aim of improving the quality of healthcare delivery, enhancing the health status of individuals and populations, lowering the costs of care delivery, and decreasing the risks and actualities of avoidable patient harm and liability losses will be covered throughout Chapters 4 through 7, appearing below. But first, there follows a primer in Chapter 3 on what is required to demonstrate medical liability. The medico-legal construct deriving from this primer will serve as the prism through which the various new financing and delivery models and their supporting technologies will need to pass to help to achieve the Quadruple Aim.

Chapter 3

MEDICAL LIABILITY IN A TECHNOLOGY-DRIVEN POST-REFORM HEALTHCARE MARKETPLACE

WHAT ELEMENTS MUST BE PROVED IN MEDICAL LIABILITY ACTIONS

Medical liability actions come under the broader area of civil law known as "torts". A tort is a civil wrong (i.e. one not requiring the violation of a criminal statute, although torts may also arise from such violations) committed either by an individual, group of individuals or corporation (the "defendant") against another individual, group of individuals or corporation (the "plaintiff").

To recover damages in a medical liability action (as with all torts), the injured (and/or otherwise aggrieved) plaintiff bringing the action must be able to prove to either a judge (who may function as both the "trier of law" and the "trier of facts") or a jury (always just the" trier of facts") by the "preponderance" of the evidence the following elements:

- *Relationship:* There must be some kind of explicit or implicit relationship between the plaintiff(s) and the defendant(s) at the time of the alleged wrongdoing. This relationship may be as loosely defined as one individual with another in a public place (or on a highway together, etc.);

- *Duty:* By virtue of this relationship, there must have been either an explicit or implied duty owed by the plaintiff(s) to the defendant(s) to adhere to either an explicit or implied standard of care;
- *Standard of Care:* The standard of care which derives from this relationship and resultant duty owed between the defendant(s) and plaintiff(s) must have been reasonable under the circumstances, with adherence or deviation from it being readily determinable and assignable;
- *Breach of the Standard of Care:* The defendant(s) must have deviated or breached this reasonable explicit or implied standard of care pre-existing between the plaintiff(s) and defendant(s) who owed that duty to adhere to that standard of care to the plaintiff(s);
- *Causation:* The action (or inaction in claims of failure to perform an action which the defendant should have executed to protect the safety of the plaintiff) must have been both the direct and proximate cause of the claimed injury to the plaintiff. The *direct cause* is that which was a necessary (i.e. a "but for this happening there would likely have been no injury") cause. The *proximate cause* is that occurrence which was the closest event in terms of actual physical proximity or nearness in time (when there may have been multiple causes) of the plaintiff's alleged injuries. It may also have been that cause which may have been reasonably foreseen as setting into motion a series of events which ultimately resulted in the plaintiff's injury. For a cause to be considered "proximate", there also could not have been any intervening causes of a negligent nature by another party, including by the plaintiff himself or herself (or themselves). There also could not have been any other superseding non-negligently generated acts or forces, including "Acts of God"; and
- *Damages:* The breach of the duty to adhere to the appropriate standard of care owed by the defendant(s) to the plaintiff(s) must have been the direct and proximate cause (as defined above) of the damages resulting from the injury alleged by the defendant. This injury must have produced measurable and recoverable past, present and/or projected future damages of a physical, economic and/or emotional nature. Such damages may include (but not be limited to): pain and suffering, loss of function, rehabilitation and/or long term care costs, or loss of occupation, reputation, consortium, or enjoyment of life. These compensable damages would not have occurred but for the negligent acts or omissions of the defendant(s).

Physicians (and others in the healthcare industry) have been loath to make it easier for plaintiffs to recover damages in medical liability actions. They and their counsel have done everything possible to avoid helping plaintiffs (their former, or even current, patients) in even the slightest way to prove the elements required to litigate these actions successfully. Critics claim that the entire $3 trillion healthcare industry has (until recently—please see Chapter 8) engaged in a "conspiracy of silence" to protect their members from liability actions. Because most patients and their families have been artificially insulated from the bulk of the costs of care, there has not been so urgent or loud a call for transparency of process and results.

All that has been (and will continue to be) changing dramatically. Please refer to all of the reasons for this as previously discussed in Chapters 1 and 2 above. Patients and their families, now function as consumers and customers as they bear an increasing proportion of medical costs. They will demand both cost and quality (i.e. transparency) information concerning the "relative value" of the healthcare services they receive and, increasingly, help finance. They will expect this transparency to help them choose the right health plan (through the health insurance exchanges or through their employee benefits plans). They will also expect much more transparency to help them to extract optimal value from the appropriate, effective and efficient diagnosis and treatment of their conditions by their physicians and other providers.

Policymakers will also demand and expect to receive transparent information about the relative cost effectiveness of providers taking part in various Medicare accountable care initiatives (e.g. the Shared Savings Program, Pioneer ACO program and Advanced Payment Initiative, among others). They will also expect and demand this level of accounting and accountability for the four different federal bundled payment programs and medical homes and neighborhoods the government may help to subsidize.

Health plans' relative value will be constantly assessed by patients functioning as consumers, as well as by purchasers (employers, unions, governmental entities and policymakers). Consequently, payers will also demand and expect useable and useful information about the relative quality and cost effectiveness of their contracted providers. By doing so, they will be able to select (and deselect) hospitals and physicians for their networks. This will be necessary to keep their plans' price, quality and overall value competitive. Achieving this will also be required for these plans to remain profitable, as they also take on even more risk (sometimes shared with providers, while other times on their own).

Again, it is (and will be increasingly) the three forces of economics, technology and data which will drive the healthcare cost and quality (value) transparency movement. The changing economics of healthcare for patients functioning as consumers will be the primary driver. However, the increasingly sophisticated technologies available and the unprecedented stores of data becoming available for analysis and performance reporting will serve as the necessary enablers to propel this movement forward.

Although perhaps not initially, but certainly, eventually, the health insurance exchanges enabled through the ACA will champion healthcare value demonstration transparency. The government's facilitating value based market competition between and among health plans lies at the heart of what the ACA is trying to accomplish. Its most important purpose is to improve the (currently woeful) ROI Americans are receiving from the $3 trillion healthcare industry in this country.

The *Platinum, Gold, Silver, and Bronze ("metallic") health plans* offered through the exchanges (offering 90, 80, 70 and 60%, respectively, for each policyholder of the overall actuarially determined healthcare costs per year by way of financial benefit) have reset the table for those partaking in the exchanges. Although intended to be primarily for individuals not receiving their health insurance coverage through their employers, an increasing number of employers are considering thrusting their previously insured-through-the-workplace employees into this market. Dr. Ezekiel Emmanuel, Vice Provost and Chair of Health Policy and Management at the University of Pennsylvania and an author of the ACA for the Obama Administration, has predicted that by 2025 all but 20% of employees will receiving their health insurance through the exchanges.

[18] *Emmanuel, E, Reinventing American Healthcare: How the Affordable Care Act will Improve our Terribly Complex, Blatantly Unjust, Outrageously Expensive, Grossly Inefficient, Error Prone System; Available from Public Affairs, a Member of the Perseus Books Group (2014)*

These previously employer-covered employees may receive subsidies from their employers to cover the costs of purchasing insurance on the exchange. However, these additional individuals (who previously had always been accustomed to having their employer pick up the lion's share of the bill) will soon become very motivated (and sophisticated) value purchasers.

They will absolutely demand information about their premium costs (by metallic plan) and the projected out of pocket costs annually for deductibles, copayment and coinsurance. They will also want to know the ROI of all these (often new and/or increased) expenditures for their and their families' healthcare. They will want to know (for themselves) at least as much about the quality, efficiency, cost effectiveness, clinical outcomes and other results of the care that they will be receiving from these various plans as their employers ever did. Their employers may have been content to receive aggregated analyses and reports of quality, efficiency, cost effectiveness, clinical outcomes and other results at a population level. However, individuals will expect and demand this level of transparency for their own individual care and its results as well as for their family members.

In addition to this new group of formerly employer-covered consumers expecting this level of increased transparency from their health plans, so too will those who had been eligible for participation in the exchanges all along. To compete effectively, health plans competing on the exchanges will also expect and demand this increasing level of transparency from all of their contracted providers. Once the flood gate for transparency opens, the flow will only increase. So how then, will this dramatically increasing transparency about the quality and cost of healthcare impact the prospects and actualities of medical liability and the relative ease or difficulty to prove the elements required to demonstrate that?

Proving Medical Liability Actions in a Technology-Transformed Healthcare Marketplace

The Relationship between Plaintiff(s) and Defendant(s)

Could the demanded greater transparency in healthcare delivery and financing transactions between patients, their families and their providers impact the nature of the relationship between the parties themselves and the potential for medical liability? The whole point of increased transparency throughout the healthcare system is to reveal what may have been previously hidden (intentionally or unintentionally) from patients and their families. This includes who is doing what to them, when, where, how and, most importantly, why.

Often, it may not be clear to a patient (who may be unconscious or heavily sedated), or even to fully conscious and non-sedated family members, what is the nature of a relationship with a provider at a specific time. In this author's own experience when one of his family members was hospitalized, there was a nice lady who religiously brought at 6 p.m. every evening a (non-prescribed) cup of nutritional supplement. Nobody on the hospital floor knew why she was bringing this supplement on any given day to my family member, much less for six straight days. But, since nobody stopped her, she continued to bring this cup of supplement into the room every day at exactly 6 p.m. for six consecutive days.

The lady (who always smiled at all of us) did not speak any English. So, we didn't question her in what she was doing. My family member never drank the supplement on any of the six days she delivered it—so, no harm, no foul. As a matter of fact, watching this play out over six straight days at exactly the same time actually became a much-needed source of amusement and stress relief for all of us. Still, at minimum, this ritual represented a waste of time, human and financial resources. At worst, however, the supplement may actually have been intended for another patient. It might have contained substances that could have harmed my family member and/or increased the time and cost of recovery.

In this case, was there an established provider-patient relationship between this nice (but apparently misguided) lady and my family member? What if what she had brought my family member to drink (perhaps intended for another patient) had been harmful? Was there a pre-existing relationship at the time of the harm? Presumably, she was a hospital employee (although we didn't even know that for sure at the time, nor did anybody else on the floor).

This occurred with all of us present, conscious and non-sedated (including my family member who was a patient). However, suppose that this had occurred in the middle of the night or at a time when my family member was alone and sedated and did not know not to drink the supplement (whether it had been harmful or not).

In teaching hospitals, the mind reels when thinking of how many newly minted physicians-in-training are permitted to diagnose and treat patients, especially in the wee hours of the morning when nobody else is around. They may have little more than a somewhat better trained, but probably inadequately focused and rested, supervising resident or fellow to sign off on their diagnostic and therapeutic plans. Hopefully, more full time board-certified hospitalists and intensivists who can be present around the clock may alleviate this concern in the future. But, there still is the transparency issue concerning the nature of the relationship: Who is the provider who owes the duty to adhere to the standard of care at any particular point in the patient's course (whether in an acute setting or elsewhere)?

Furthermore, as technology begins to play an increasingly important role in the diagnosis and treatment of patients, what will be the relationship between these technologies and patients? For example, what will be the relationship between physicians and patients in a remotely monitored ICU (an e-ICU), or, for that matter, in any telemedicine encounter or virtual patient care visit? What will be the relationship (and the duty to adhere to the standard of care) between patients and medical robots? What about the nature of the relationship between patients and Dr. Watson (or any number of other electronic diagnostic and therapeutic decision making aides)? Is there (or will there soon be) definable and legally enforceable relationships established between patients and the full panoply of technologies (any of which could malfunction and result in both directly and proximately caused harm)? Further discussion of these potential relationships and the duties and standards of care arising from them follows below.

Duties Owed by the Defendant(s) to the Plaintiff(s)

What impact will demands on greater transparency in future healthcare transactions have on the particular nature and extent of the duty owed by defendant(s) to plaintiff(s)? Probably the biggest change will derive from the fact that, for lack of a better term, "machines" will be playing a much bigger role in healthcare delivery and patients' clinical outcomes in the years and decades ahead. Consequently, there will be new duties of expected, reasonable care owed not only from physicians and other human providers of care, but also by the "machines". These duties will be owed by those who have designed, manufactured, packaged, delivered, used, supervised, managed or otherwise controlled the use of such "machines" in the delivery of healthcare.

These "thinking machines" will function increasingly like artificial life forms (more closely than ever approximating, and even improving upon, human intelligence). Might a duty of care to patients even be imposed on these machines, independent of their manufacturers and users? If that sounds like science fiction right now, just think about the "internet of all things". Among an infinite number of other possibilities, with the "internet of all things", refrigerators can now inform you when your milk is about to go bad. Imagine, how that may have sounded even a decade ago.

Products liability law (including legal theories of duties owed such as "implied warranty of fitness" or even strict liability for any "defects") has already been out there for decades. However, legal precedents may either not apply (or will need to be reshaped) to cover the newer technologies. For example, what will be the nature and extent of the duty owed by a manufacturer of an electronic health record system (with embedded computerized physician order entry and clinical decision support) that malfunctions? In some cases, products liability law may be applicable. Suppose an EHR contains clearly identifiable software glitches so that physician orders for one patient get miscommunicated by the software to be for another patient. In that case, at least the implied warranty of fitness for a particular purpose (if not strict liability for a product defect) might well apply.

However, what if the embedded clinical decision support system (CDSS) works as it is supposed to do, but the medical evidentiary base driving its algorithms is outdated? Does the physician (or other provider treating a patient, and potential plaintiff) have a duty to ensure that the suggestions followed are based on the absolute, most leading edge, double blinded, controlled clinical trial evidence? What is the duty of the manufacturer of the EHR (with these embedded CDSS) to make sure of that?

Does a physician (or other treating provider) have a duty to install the CDSS (as part of the EHR)? Does a physician (or other treating provider) have a duty not to set the thresholds for a CDSS firing alerts too high, so that alerts not to use particular drugs or other treatments based on each patient's individual clinical characteristics rarely are triggered? Does the provider have a duty to learn how to use the CDSS functionality effectively so that it can demonstrably improve the quality and safety of care while not interfering with clinical workflow?

Does the provider have a duty not to ignore the recommendations of the CDSS? Does the provider have a duty to ignore the recommendations of the CDSS if he (or she) knows (or should know) that the evidentiary base from which they derive is outdated (or is otherwise inaccurate or insufficient given the particular nature of a patient's condition and illness severity, including contraindications to follow the advice given)? How much of each patient's genetic predispositions to respond well (or not well, even catastrophically, to particular recommendations from the CDSS) do provider users of these systems owe a duty to each patient to know and to use in their care? If the EHR has access to each patient's genomic and proteomic database, can (or should) physicians rely on the CDSS' ability to incorporate this complex information into its recommendations to treat (or not treat) patients in a certain way?

The whole point of CDSS is to extend dramatically providers' individual and collective abilities (and memories) to bring to bear the best possible personalized care for every patient based on their conditions, illness severities, and genetic susceptibilities. However, if physicians and other providers have to know as much or more about all the medical evidentiary bases on which these machines' diagnostic and/or therapeutic algorithms are based, then what additional value do they really confer? Providers might quite reasonably come to the conclusion that they should not go to all the trouble to evaluate, purchase, install and use these technologies, if doing so might actually increase the extent of their potential liabilities to patients.

One of the most complex areas of medical malpractice law in the years and decades ahead will center on how to define and assign the nature and extent of the duties of care owed to their patients between providers and the manufacturers (and marketers) of CDSS technologies. Building on the brief introduction of this topic in this section, how the standard of care is likely to be defined and assigned in this technology-driven world of healthcare delivery follows in the next section.

The Current and the Evolving Standard of Care

The standard of care in medical liability actions has evolved over the past 3800 years dating back to the Hammurabi Code. In that ancient law, there was a provision not unlike the "eye for an eye and a tooth for a tooth" principle of retribution found in the Old Testament. In so many words, the Code held that a surgeon responsible for killing a patient would pay with the loss of his own hands. This punishment presumably would have ended an ancient defendant surgeon's career. As big a nuisance as medical malpractice is to today's physicians, at least the consequences of deviation from currently prevailing standards of care are not quite as draconian as they were in Hammurabi's day.

In more Modern Times, the standard of care has evolved significantly, also. There are local standards of care. These might seek to answer the question of what would "reasonable and comparably trained and experienced physicians and surgeons" in that community have done in diagnosing and treating patients with similar conditions and illness severities, compared to what the defendant(s) actually did or didn't do.

There are also national standards of care. These usually derive from the best evidence based medical practices which have been adopted by national medical and surgical specialty societies. Their adoption and publication would follow only after considerable vetting and evaluating of the latest results from controlled clinical trials and other sources of medical evidence. There have often been blue ribbon panels of medical experts assembled who have had input and perhaps even the ultimate say on what goes into these best evidence based medical practices and the standards of care deriving from them.

However, even in what might be considered to be the most scrupulously evaluated best practices and standards of care, there has always been built into them exceptions justifying case by case deviations (so long as they have been appropriately documented and explained). In addition, the law has been sufficiently flexible even to permit two often conflicting "schools of thought" to coexist.

An example of competing schools of thought is the recommendation from the U.S. Preventive Services Task Force not to require mammograms in patients under 50 in the absence of a positive family history of breast cancer and/or other recognized risk factors. This differs from the recommendation of many national medical and surgical specialty societies (and the American Cancer Society). Those groups continue to recommend that all women have mammograms starting at age 40. However, a recently published long term study found that annual mammograms between the ages of 40 and 59 had no impact on mortality. Furthermore, they may even have resulted in harm to patients receiving false positive findings.

[19] *Miller, AB, et al., Twenty Five Year Follow up for Breast Cancer Incidence and Mortality of the Canadian National Breast Screening Study; Randomised Screening Trial; BMJ 2014; 348g366.*

www.bmj.com/content/348/bmj.g366

However, no matter how complex and confusing trying to divine the standard of care has been in the past, it will only get to be even more that way (perhaps exponentially) in the years and decades ahead. As the sum total of medical knowledge doubles every two years, the standard of care will need to evolve with it. In the words of cardiologist and futurist, Eric Topol, M.D.:

"We live in an extraordinary data-rich universe, a world that had only accumulated 1 billion gigabytes from the dawn of civilization until 2003. But now, we are generating multiple zettabytes—each representing 1 trillion gigabytes—each year and will exceed 35 zettabytes by 2020, roughly equivalent to the amount of data on 250 billion DVDs. Sensors are now the dominant source of worldwide-generated data with 1,250 billion gigabytes in 2010, representing more bits than all of the stars in the universe."

[17] *Topol, E, How Technology is Transforming Health Care—Digital Devices are empowering the Patient and Changing the Face of Healthcare; Excerpted from Eric Topol, "The Creative Destruction of Medicine"; Basic*

Books (2012) as reproduced in U.S News & World Report; 2014 Best Hospitals Edition; pp. 3-7 (2013).

Dr. Topol, in his book “The Creative Destruction of Medicine”, also goes on to say how the transition from single chips containing massively parallel processor arrays, to supercomputers (like Dr. Watson) with hundreds or thousands of central processing units, will make commonplace whole genome sequencing. Whole genomes may be broken into tiny pieces to determine life codes in a massively parallel fashion—please see the previous reference from Dr. Topol’s book. These new and rapidly evolving technological capabilities will permit exponential improvements in genomics, proteomics and, ultimately, “personalized medicine”. Care can be individualized for each patient based on condition, illness severity, and genetic susceptibilities to respond to specific treatments.

As a consequence of this explosion in both biomedicine and the relative abilities of information technology to analyze “Big Data”, the focus of evolving standards of care in future medical liability cases may shrink. The emphasis may devolve from that of national standards (or schools of thought) all the way down to what standard of care should have been applied to each unique individual. The question may become whether physicians (or whoever, or whatever, may be providing the bulk of care to patients in the future, including non-human entities) adhered to the best evidence based therapeutic practices. These evidence based standards may well be based not only on each patient’s particular condition and illness severity, but also their detailed genetic predispositions to respond (or not respond) to particular treatments (with optimal outcomes and minimal adverse effects).

Should future plaintiffs choose to waive their rights to privacy, exhibits in medical malpractice trials not too long from now may very well contain detailed reports of their genomic sequences that made them either good or bad candidates for the treatments defendant providers chose for them. How well future providers were able to access and analyze this genomic information about their patients prior to instituting certain treatment regimens may also become part of the standard of care to which they will need to adhere. So, in addition to understanding what these genomic sequences in particular patients mean for how they should be treated, future providers may also need to have access to massively parallel processors that can accurately (and fairly quickly) produce these reports. These reports may well need to be available to both provider and patient at the point of care. Being able to do so may very well soon constitute the standard of care to which future providers must adhere in their dealings with patients to prevent them from ever becoming plaintiffs.

Causation: Both Direct and Proximate

Causation in any medical liability action even in the relatively recent past (i.e. the 20th century) has been one of the most complex and difficult concepts to understand, much less to predict. From their first tort law class, attorneys fondly remember the classic (and unforgettable) case of poor Mrs. Palsgraf injured by a falling scales "but for" exploding fireworks which employees of the Long Island Railroad were allegedly negligent in dislodging from the grip of another passenger attempting to board a departing train.

[20] *Palsgraf v. Long Island Railroad, 28 N.Y. 339.* 162 N.E. 99 (1928).

For the sake of argument, let's assume for the minute that the employees dislodging the fireworks from the boarding passenger were negligent, and thus, so was their employer, the Railroad, through the legal principle of vicarious liability. Let's go further and posit that the exploding fireworks were the direct ("but for") cause of Mrs. Palsgraf's injuries by the scales that fell on her resulting from this explosion. Could it be said that this rather bizarre turn of events was foreseeable? To be the proximate cause, what ultimately occurred needs to be a foreseeable consequence of the breach of the duty of care to Mrs. Palsgraf which was the direct ("but for") cause of her injury.

Although this case was ultimately decided at the Court of Appeals level in New York in favor of the defendant (after having gone against the Railroad in two lower level state courts), there were three (out of seven) dissenting judges. Many future plaintiffs have cited persuasively and successfully in their own cases the reasoning behind the strong dissent from Judge Andrews (affirming the judgments of the two lower courts). That dissent reasoned that a defendant's demonstrably negligent act (or, in some cases, an omission of an act owed as a duty to the plaintiff to perform) could be regarded as both the required direct *and* proximate cause of an injury to even an unforeseen plaintiff. Mrs. Palsgraf was such an unforeseen plaintiff. Also, her injuries were unforeseen (and precisely how they came about even less foreseeable). Nevertheless, by Judge Andrews' reasoning, negligently dislodging the fireworks of another passenger had the potential to result in possible injury to others (whoever they may be and however unforeseeable the nature of or particular way by which that harm occurred might be). In other words, it is enough for *some* type of harm to befall even unforeseeable plaintiffs in unforeseeable ways that could be reasonably expected to have occurred as a result of a negligent act or omission for the proximate causation requirement to be met.

Imagine then for a minute how plaintiffs' attorneys try to use Judge Andrews' often successfully cited persuasive reasoning for proving direct and proximate causation in medical liability actions in the post-reform, technology-driven healthcare landscape painted thus far. Think about the complexities of proving direct and proximate causation in medical liability cases in years past. Then multiply that complexity exponentially to get an idea of how it will be in the not too distant future. A non-exhaustive list of possibilities concerning what kinds of breaches in the standard of care (acts or omissions) that could be seen as direct and proximate causes might include:

- Injuries resulting from the failure of physicians or other providers to turn on and/or use and act upon the results from the diagnostic decision making capabilities (e.g. Isabel or Dr. Watson) embedded in electronic health record systems;
- Injuries resulting from the failure of physicians or other providers to turn on and/or use and act upon the results from the evidence-based treatment algorithms in the clinical decision support systems embedded in electronic health record systems;
- Injuries resulting from the failure of physicians or other providers to access through the cloud and/or other available interoperable health information exchanges complete patient information at the point of care;
- Injuries resulting from the failure of physicians or other providers to access complete genomic and proteomic information on patients prior to instituting treatments. These patients may have had genetic susceptibilities to adverse reactions which could have been revealed through these prior analyses;
- Injuries resulting from the failure of physicians or other providers to heed a whole host of clinical alerts such as adverse drug-drug, drug-disease, drug-lab result, or other reactions. These may have resulted due to either not installing these safety protecting feature, ignoring the alerts (since the threshold for firing was set too low), or setting the threshold too high for them to fire (except for the most life threatening reactions); and/or
- Injuries resulting from the failure of physicians or other providers to heed and prevail upon their patients to undergo preventive medicine screenings for a full range of cancers, high cholesterol, blood pressure/stroke risk, etc.

There are more examples of potential liability deriving from injuries to patients/plaintiffs owing to failure to fully use the quality and safety-enhancing functionalities of electronic health records and other information technologies. Some of these may be found in the previously cited publication:

[8] *Princeton Insurance. Electronic medical record patient safety and risk management guide. Princeton, NJ (2009).* http://www.pinsco.com/downloads/EMRUsersGuide_final.pdf.

Compensable Damages

Damages (at least those that are compensable) are the last piece of the puzzle plaintiffs must be able to prove to recover in medical liability actions (as with all tort actions). There are many types of damages that may (or may not) be compensable. A non-exhaustive list would include:

- Past (immediate post-injury), present and projected future *Medical Costs* (inpatient, outpatient, sub-acute and chronic care facilities' costs, rehabilitation, physician and other practitioner costs, drug and imaging costs, lab and other diagnostic aid costs, medical equipment costs, home care costs, etc.);
- Past (immediate post-injury), present and projected future *Economic Costs* (loss of wages and salaries, loss of livelihood/career, loss of professional reputation, loss of pensions and retirement benefits and other direct and indirect consequences of not being able to work or to seek work);
- *Pain and Suffering* (from the time of the injury forward which may often constitute the bulk of the overall damages award). These damages may include loss of consortium, loss of enjoyment of past activities, unrelenting pain interfering with all aspects of functioning in various roles as a worker, spouse, parent, community member, etc.; and
- *Punitive Damages (*which may be awarded in cases of particularly egregious and/or reckless behavior or misconduct directly resulting in the aggrieved party's injuries). When these are awarded, these too may rival or even surpass pain and suffering as the largest component of damages awards.

What is important to grasp about these different types of damages is that for any of them to be awarded, they must be "compensable". To be "compensable", damages must be proven by the preponderance of the evidence to have flowed directly from demonstrable injuries. These injuries must have resulted from the defendant(s) breach of the standard of care owed to the plaintiff, as the direct and proximate cause of such breach. The duty to comply with the standard of care must have arisen from a specific, definable, established relationship between the parties. All these elements must be proven by the preponderance of the evidence for the plaintiff to recover damages (of any type or to any extent).

Consider the types and extent of compensable damages now in the cauldron of the rapidly evolving current and future technology-driven healthcare reform brew laid out above. The different types and extent of damages may stay roughly similar to how they have been in the past, on the one hand. On the other hand, what likely will change will be the scope of what is compensable based on what can be demonstrated by the preponderance of the evidence as having flowed directly from the harm negligently caused.

For example, suppose a patient can demonstrate injury that is the direct and proximate cause (as explained above) of the failure to take fully into account complete genomic and proteomic information about his or her relative susceptibilities to particular treatments. If, as a result, the patient's outcomes turned out to be suboptimal, what would be the compensable damages? Would the damages be measured by comparing the actual clinical outcome of the patient versus what could or should have been achievable, had the patient's treatment been more "personalized".

If the damage claimed was the "loss of a chance" to recover from an otherwise fatal condition, then comparing that result (i.e. death) to the presumably preferable alternative (i.e. life), might be fairly clear cut. However, suppose that the damages claimed were those attributable to achieving merely a "tolerable" versus an anticipated outstanding result? That calculus has been the basis for many claims arising from allegedly "suboptimal" plastic surgical procedures (at least among current and aspiring models)

Let's assume for the moment that failing to produce an optimally achievable result (with the technological and communication resources that will become increasingly accessible in the future in medical transactions) could be found to constitute a breach in the standard of care. One of the most prevalent (if not compelling) reason for patients (or anybody) to sue in the first place is a failure for a result deriving from a transaction in a relationship to meet their expectations (whether those expectations were reasonable or not). As the "New Medicine" moves us toward "designer genes" (if not "designer people"), what types and extents of failures to achieve those ideals may justify the awarding of damages? Consider these queries:

May parents (and/or their kids) sue and recover "compensable damages" on behalf of their (allegedly world class athletic) children whose providers don't deliver the latest personalized treatments for their asthma? These parents might claim that not doing so deprived their offspring of the chance to receive full ride college athletic scholarships. Even assuming that all of the other elements of the liability action could be proven (including that these athletes would have been good enough to have earned full ride scholarships had they received the more "personalized" medical treatments), should these "damages" be ruled "compensable"?

The loss of "full ride college scholarships" could amount to up to a quarter million dollars today and multiples of that in the decades ahead. However, what if the claimed loss was that of not acquiring a long term professional sports contracts (which could amount to tens or even hundreds of millions of dollars even today)?

The capabilities of the "New Medicine" may bring us closer not only to the essential cures of previously fatal diseases, but also to the optimization of the human condition. However, what may be the limits of "compensable damages" for failing to achieve that ideal in the future? These questions may not be ones that physicians and other providers (or their current or future defense counsel) may wish to contemplate. However, they can be sure that inventive plaintiffs' attorneys (and their current and future clients) will be.

Chapter 4

The Shifting Focus of Medical Liability in a Value-Driven System

Accountable Care—Its Name Alone May Carry Increased Liability Implications

To be "accountable" has become a mantra in both the public and private sectors of late. This has been especially true since the financial crisis of 2008 and the Great Recession (almost Great Depression 2.0) from which our country is still not fully recovered. It was the financial services industry for which the phrase "being held accountable" has had its greatest resonance over the past six years. However, the same applies (or should apply) to a $3 trillion healthcare system that has been out of control for the past *sixty* years. This has been the case since third party payment and first dollar coverage fee for service became perceived as a birthright for Americans, especially for members in big unions, starting back in the early 1950s.

Skeptics regard "accountable care" as the latest reincarnation of the discredited managed care revolution of the 1980s and 1990s rearing its ugly head once again--this time driven by the federal government. They believe that this is just another wolf in sheep's clothing whose real purpose is to save money and drive down hospital and physician reimbursement. To seem altruistic, provider critics claim that it will be their patients (not themselves) who will be most hurt and inconvenienced by accountable care. They claim it will decrease their patients' choice of hospitals and physicians (through so-called "narrow networks") and subject their personal medical information to more probing.

These critics are really not wrong. One of the goals of accountable care *is* certainly to decrease costs. One of the better ways to do this may be through the imposition of narrow hospital and physician networks, so long as those who qualify for inclusion are delivering demonstrably superior value care to patients. There *is* a much greater focus on quality in accountable care organizations or ACOs--both in those sponsored by the public and well as the private sector. Failure to meet quality goals may substantially reduce, if not eliminate altogether, the opportunity for providers to share in savings for having taken care of a specific population of patients for less money in a given time period than what was originally projected and appropriated.

A comprehensive explanation of all the different types of accountable care organizations (hereafter ACOs), their quality goal standards, financial upside and downside risk structures, payment methodologies, delivery models and incentive systems is outside the scope of this book. Regardless of the various forms that ACOs might take, however, their overriding purpose is to improve both the quality *and* cost effectiveness (i.e. the demonstrable *value)* of healthcare delivery. It is the ACOs' quality goals (which either must be met to share savings and/or toward meeting which goals, tangible, continuous improvement must be demonstrable), which carry the greatest medical legal implications.

The analysis in Chapter 3 covered what needs to be proven by the preponderance of the evidence to result in successful medical liability actions. Could it be concluded that failure to meet or exceed all of an ACO's quality goals could rise to the level of a breach in the standard of care owed to all patients for whose care those participating providers are to be held "accountable"? Are these quality goals aspirational--or the minimal--which should be met to achieve the standard of care? If so, is this a medical standard of care? Alternatively, for the purposes of deciding liability in cases arising in ACOs, could meeting these quality requirements constitute a *legal* standard of care? Must *all* of the quality goals be met (especially in those ACO arrangements which are so-called "all or nothing" in which all these goals must be met for participants to share in savings)? If not all of the goals need to be met to share in savings, would failure to meet any of those quality goals that *were* required to be met to share in savings constitute a breach in the standard of care?

Suppose there had been measurable improvement toward meeting quality goals (whether minimal or aspirational) that *did* need to be met to share in savings. Would that be enough to say that the standard of care had been met? Would evidence of this improvement (or lack thereof) in meeting these quality standards even be admissible into evidence? There *is* the public policy of not admitting into evidence in liability actions interventions taken to improve public safety where failure to do so could result in negligently inflicted injury. These are just some of the medical legal issues that will surround ACOs. They will need to be resolved once plaintiffs who were patients being treated in the context of ACOs begin to bring medical liability actions.

VALUE BASED PURCHASING AND INSURANCE DESIGN

Probably the most powerful transformative change beginning to occur in the $3 trillion healthcare industry is the movement from reimbursing for volume to rewarding for demonstrable value. This is the essence of value based purchasing (hereafter VBP) and its counterpart directly focused on improving the health of consumers of care: value based insurance design (VBID).

"The current, predominant, fee for service reimbursement system continues to severely fragment the delivery and financing of care. It drives up its costs (since one person's waste is another person's profit). It divorces responsibility for the financial consequences of bad health and clinical decisions by patients and providers alike. It creates the false impression that 'more care is somehow better care'".

[21] *Couch, J.B., Value-Based Purchasing at 25: Looking Back & Looking Ahead; in: Stephano, RM, Edelheit, J, Engaging Wellness: Corporate Wellness Programs that Work; pp. 530-1; Corporate Health and Wellness Association; Palm Beach Gardens, FL (2012).*

The false impression that "more care is better care" has been at the heart of the mythology of American medical practice since the third party fee for service reimbursement system really took off after World War II. This myth has also been a huge driver of the entire medical liability industry and the up to 10% of the $3 trillion dollar healthcare industry attributable to defensive medical practices.

[22] *The Price of Excess: Identifying Waste in Healthcare Spending; PricewaterhouseCoopers Health Research Institute (2008).*

However, defensive medical practices not only do not prevent physicians and other providers from getting sued, they actually increase the risks and realities of this happening. Before getting further into that, let's examine more fully the impact to the entire industry (not just the prospects for medical liability) that the move from reimbursing for volume to rewarding for demonstrable value will likely have.

VBP (in an explicit, albeit still embryonic form) began in the 1980s. Its earliest actual health policy application was in the initial work of the Pennsylvania Healthcare Cost Containment Council (PHC4) as recounted in the first article to use this term (or one similar to it)

[23] *Couch, J.B., Medical Care Value Purchasing: Why Now and How to Prepare for It; DRG Monitor; 1987; 4(9):1-8.*

"This article on medical care value purchasing discussed how the Pennsylvania Healthcare Cost Containment Council (known then and now as PHC4) attempted to establish a value driven market way back in the 1980s. Large employers were to purchase healthcare services (through health plans, and, perhaps, even directly from hospitals and physician groups) based on their demonstrable value. Quality and cost effectiveness were to be assessed by the clinical outcomes and financial costs of treating patients with specific conditions and undergoing particular procedures. These outcomes were to be compared to what would be expected for these parameters based on patients' pretreatment severity of illness as measured by a proprietary system, the MedisGroups System by MediQual Systems, of Westborough, MA. The employer-dominated PHC4 mandated that all 307 hospitals in Pennsylvania obtain, implement and use this software system for these purposes."

[21] *Cf. generally, Couch, JB, Value Based Purchasing at 25 at 531*

In November, 1987, a follow up article on medical care value purchasing comprehensively developed its core principles and practices concerning how it should work in the healthcare delivery and financing system:

"For medical care value purchasing (as well as VBP) to work, the following needs to be in place:

- Definitions of provider quality and cost-effectiveness mutually agreed upon by providers and purchasers;
- Systems for measuring provider quality and cost-effectiveness mutually agreed upon by providers and purchasers;
- Standards mutually agreed upon by providers and purchasers against which severity-adjusted provider quality and cost-effectiveness could be compared;
- Criteria mutually agreed upon by providers and purchasers for selecting providers on the basis of their measured clinical performance as compared to these standards;

- The redesign of healthcare benefit programs to create incentives to channel subscribers toward high value providers and away from low value providers; and
- Methods to establish and continually adjust provider reimbursement levels on the basis of the demonstrated value of their healthcare services to subscribers."

  [24] Couch, Medical Care Value Purchasing; Update and Emerging Applications; DRG Monitor; 1987; 5(3):1-8

Over a quarter century later, there are still very few places in this country where health care purchasing, financing and delivery systems are firing on all six of these VBP cylinders. At least partially because of its widespread failure to follow these VBP principles and practices, the U.S., in a survey conducted by the Commonwealth Fund, recently came in dead last among the 11 most advanced industrialized nations in the world in terms of care quality, patient outcomes and overall health. The U.S. also came in a very strong first place (by more than a 50% margin over second place Norway) for per capita costs. This represents a kind of complete "Anti-Triple Aim" result (and probably would be a complete "Anti-Quadruple Aim" result if medical liability rates and expenses had also been surveyed). The least expensive healthcare system (at barely more than a third--$3405—of the U.S. per capita costs for 2011 of $8508) was the oft-maligned United Kingdom's National Health Service, or U.K. NHS. Past praise for the U.K. NHS by the nation's foremost "Triple Aim" advocate, Donald Berwick, M.D., M.P.P., cost him any Republican support for getting confirmed in the U.S. Senate to be a "permanent" CMS Administrator. Even more significantly, the U.K. also moved up to first place in terms of quality (based on 2013 responses) in this most recent survey. Dr. Karen Davis, Professor of Health Policy and Management at Johns Hopkins University, and Former CEO of the Commonwealth Fund for 20 years, authored this report. It was the lead health story of the day in many of the top national periodicals and journals, e.g. the "Washington Post":

[25] *Bernstein, L, Once Again, U.S. has Most Expensive, Least Effective Health Care System in Survey; Washington Post (Online); June 16, 2014.* http://wapo.st/1kX4ZNz.

This very recent survey from probably the most highly respected and experienced healthcare foundation in the world in the area of comparing leading nations' healthcare systems shows how far the U.S. has yet to go. Over the course of the past 10 years (as noted in four separate surveys by the Commonwealth Fund), the U.S. has failed to move up in these quality rankings (while substantially increasing its lead in terms of per capita costs). Most other countries have moved up significantly in terms of patients' perception of quality, outcomes and overall health, while remaining far below the U.S. in terms of per capita cost. Consequently, the perceived value of the U.S. Healthcare System has sunk abysmally compared to that of the other 10 most highly industrialized and advanced nations evaluated in this just-released survey.

But what role does (and should) the patient have in this very embarrassing result for the U.S. healthcare system? The next section of this chapter concerns how patients (and/or their families) need to get themselves much more actively engaged to try to improve the value of healthcare delivery, their outcomes and overall health results.

HOW DOES VBID DIFFER FROM VBP?

"Technically, at least the health benefits redesign part of value based insurance design (VBID), is a part of VBP—see bulleted criteria # 5 cited in reference # 24, above. However, it differs from VBP's major focus. VBP concentrates on how purchasers and payers may evaluate and incent providers to improve the quality, safety and efficiency (i.e. value) of care from the patients' payers' and purchasers' perspectives. VBID, on the other hand, focuses on how to get patients (whether employees, dependents, or retirees) to make better healthcare decisions. These better decisions may improve their own health through lifestyle and other behavior modifications. Their better decisions may also improve their health by purchasing and using more cost effective medicine and other treatments. VBID also helps patients to seek care from superior value providers and obtain that care in the least expensive, yet safe and effective, care setting (which goal *is* covered by the fifth component of VBP, as articulated, above).

VBID involves providing the financial and non-financial incentives to patients and their families to nudge them toward these healthier choices and cost effective alternatives to managing their conditions. VBP focuses on providing both financial and non-financial incentives to stimulate providers to continuously evaluate and improve the quality, safety and efficiency of care they deliver to individuals and populations of patients, whose medical and healthcare costs payers and purchasers help to finance." [21] Cf., generally, *Couch, J.B., Value Based Purchasing at 25 at 536-7*

What are the potential medical liability implications arising from this transformational shift from reimbursing for volume to continuously evaluating and rewarding providers for demonstrable value? This value will be determined increasingly by those who pay for and receive care. Increasingly, the patient/consumer will fulfill both those roles.

Begin by considering the myth that "more care is better care". For this country to make the necessary transition from volume to value, this myth needs to be thoroughly debunked. Its currently corrosive impact on the quality and cost effectiveness (i.e. value) of care through its fueling of wasteful and counterproductive defensive medical practices is discussed immediately below.

DEFENSIVE MEDICINE: ITS COUNTERPRODUCTIVE AND HARMFUL EFFECTS

Physicians (especially those trained in the pre-DRG era), from their earliest days in medical school, learned that they should consider every *conceivable* diagnosis based on patients' symptoms and other information. The fee for service system enabled, if not promoted, this mindset. Fledgling physicians were encouraged to recommend a blizzard of tests, procedures and consultations no matter how unnecessary, invasive, unsafe and expensive to the system (and, increasingly, nowadays, for patients and their families). They were taught that this was necessary to be able to rule in or rule out each and every possible diagnosis. They came to believe that doing so was in the interests of patients, furthered the intellectual process of clinical decision making, and ultimately promoted optimal medical care. In reality, this type of approach accomplished none of those goals, and actually increased (unnecessarily) the risks (and realities) of medical errors, suboptimal clinical outcomes, runaway costs and increased liability.

Diagnostic and therapeutic decision making are processes. All processes have discrete steps to execute. As explained earlier, the Six Sigma Process Improvement discipline teaches that for every step of every process there are opportunities for error, and a certain percentage likelihood that errors in the exercise of each step may (and do) occur. The opportunities for errors (and the actual number of errors) goes up not just arithmetically, but geometrically (if not exponentially), as steps are added to processes. Every time that yet another possible (as opposed to probable) diagnosis is added to the list to rule in or rule out, that compels physicians (and those carrying out their orders) to greatly complicate the diagnostic decision making process by adding a huge number of tests, procedures and consultations.

Usually, the sole purpose of consultation requests to specialists and subspecialists is for them to undertake (often invasive) procedures. These procedures have their own risks and limitations, which are often not taken sufficiently into account relative to such procedures' positive predictive value. The many lab tests done (routinely and often unnecessarily on patients) carry their own limitations in terms of their inherent sensitivities, specificities, positive and negative predictive values. All these factors further complicate the diagnostic process and increase dramatically the opportunities for and realities of medical errors. This is not even to mention the greatly added costs to patients, insurers, employers, the government, and the overall health system.

However, because in the fee for service world, these tests, procedures and consultations were all reimbursed (at least to some unspecified and often unknowable extent), medical economics continued to be served. Even if physicians did not continue to be rewarded for ordering all these tests, procedures, and consultations, they still could justify this approach. They could do so because of their strong belief that this was the best way to practice medicine. They could also rationalize that to avoid potential liability, they needed to rule out even the most unlikely (but still conceivable) diagnoses.

Nevertheless, here is how that continuing mindset and approach actually *increases* the chances for medical liability. The biggest reason for litigation is the breakdown in the physician-patient relationship. This breakdown begins to occur as soon as physicians start to regard patients as potential plaintiffs (and not as vulnerable people who are scared and looking for compassionate care). To protect themselves (not to help their patients), they order a wide array of costly and invasive tests, procedures and consultations to rule in or rule out many diagnoses that were merely possible, but not all that likely. Patients and their families can sense that physicians are doing this more to protect themselves legally. This accelerates the breakdown in their relationship.

This is just the beginning of what has flowed from taking this approach to clinical decision making. Focusing on *all possible* vs. the *most probable* explanations for patients' symptoms makes it much more likely that there will be false positives. These false positives lead to additional unnecessary, and, often, even more invasive, risky and costly procedures. This exponentially increases the likelihood and actualities of error, as well as the risks of injuries simply from the execution of these procedures, alone.

Finally, there are the added costs. As an increasing portion of medical expenses are passed onto patients, they and their families have to take on much greater costs. Enduring a period of weeks (or even months) to complete all these tests, procedures and consultations (often in multiple institutions and other care settings), patients and their families may become increasingly aggravated.

It is the disparity between their expectations and the actual results that patients experience that is a second leading stimulator for patients to sue. Their relationship with their physicians may have already deteriorated throughout this prolonged process. This makes it more likely that for each additional test, procedure, consultation and amount of time involved, their expectations for good, if not optimal, clinical outcomes rises significantly. So these two fundamental causes of increased liability risk actually feed each other to make it much more likely that patients will sue for suboptimal clinical results.

If a patient *does* sue because his or her physician(s) actually *did* miss an obscure diagnosis, having undertaken all these defensive medical practices could *possibly* provide some protection during the litigation process itself. However, taking the defensive approach to patient care outlined above will only *increase* the risks of getting sued *in the first place*. Any physician can tell you, getting sued (even if the case is settled the next day for nothing), costs a lot psychologically, if not professionally and economically.

How may VBP and VBID impact (or be impacted by) the medical liability construct outlined in Chapter 3? The following section of this chapter begins that discussion.

How VBP and VBID May Be Undertaken from a Medical Legal Perspective

Both VBP and VBID seek to improve the quality, safety and efficiency of healthcare delivery. That is their reason for being. They turn on its head the old "more is better" mantra inherent to volume driven fee for service medicine. It has been that volume-driven ethic that has also been the primary force behind defensive medical practices. This has given rise to relying too much on technology and taking a more "shotgun" vs "laser beam" approach to medical diagnosis and treatment.

Because this "more is better" philosophy is so firmly embedded in both the medical and medical legal psyches, any approach (like VBP and VBID) which promotes something quite different has become immediately suspect. Although fee for service medicine will (inevitably for economic as well as quality and safety reasons) give way to VBP, it will be a rough, choppy transition. What is considered to be "good medicine" according to fee for service will have to be redefined for VBP and VBID.

How to determine what constitutes high quality, safe, effective and efficient care will need to change. The key metric will need to be whether the care delivery process has improved patients' outcomes by whatever process employed (including some that may have been considered unorthodox in the past).

Metrics to determine whether patient outcomes (both at an individual and population level) improve and/or reach certain predetermined levels sufficient to trigger value based compensation will change constantly. Medico-legal standards of care will also need to evolve to keep pace. They will need to dovetail with these changing definitions of what constitutes good medical care from the perspective of VBP and VBID. However, it will be during this transition period to value-driven care (before the medical liability system and its outdated volume-driven standards of care evolve also—See Chapter 8), when there may be increased liability risks.

This increased risk in the early transition period may well stem from applying "old school" standards to care that is delivered much more economically in a VBP context. Care in this context may not achieve some predetermined "optimal standard" that theoretically (albeit not practically) could have been achieved in a fee for service context.

The topic of what constitutes "cost effective care" (which consideration will be raised in VBP evaluations) concerns itself with whether the extra cost expended to manage patients with certain conditions and illness severities is "worth it". This usually translates to a determination of how many "quality-adjusted life years" or QALYs are gained per dollar expended in treating such patients.

The problem with this medical economics approach to care is that it usually applies to populations of patients. Medical liability (almost always) concerns itself with whether care to individual patients (largely without regard to cost, let alone QALYs/Dollar) has met a particular standard of care. So, medical care in the future which is delivered pursuant to incentives inherent to driving VBP and VBID may well find itself in the middle of this dilemma. What may well have been a good clinical decision (i.e. a cost effective one for populations of patients with all factors being taken into account) could result in harm to individual patients. Plaintiffs may be able to claim successfully that at least an "old school" fee for service standard of care was violated. In fact, any argument by defense counsel that their clients didn't perform certain treatments because they hadn't met specific QALYs/Dollars thresholds would probably land with a huge "thud" (at least for the foreseeable future).

However, physicians and other practitioners will need to survive and thrive in an evolving VBP and VBID environment. They should not have to find themselves subjected to yet additional theories of liability. Medical legal standards of care must evolve in tandem with those by which the quality of care for reimbursement purposes will be determined. Those leading and managing VBP and VBID initiatives must be scrupulously careful not to imply that failure to achieve a certain level of patient outcomes (whether for individuals or populations) could ever be used as evidence that the standard of care has been violated.

The whole purpose of VBP and VBID is to provide financial and professional incentives to spur continuously improving care, patient outcomes, and efficiencies (the "Triple Aim"). However, for the "Triple Aim" not to be subverted by the medical liability system, it must evolve into a "Quadruple Aim". The fourth aim seeks also to decrease the risks and actualities of medical liability. *[9] Couch, How to Use Electronic Health Records to Achieve the Quadruple Aim; JAMA Intern Med; 173(3): 250; February 11, 2013*

VBP and VBID proponents will not want to find themselves in the dilemma of promoting superior value care which may, nevertheless, result in increased risks and actualities of medical litigation. There must be technology-driven metrics to ensure that individual (as well as population) health goals are met. How leading edge technologies (and improved patient safety and complementary risk management methods) may help achieve both these goal in a technology-driven, post reform environment will be covered in Chapter 7, below.

BUNDLED PAYMENTS

Bundled payments have been around in different forms for some years now. The most highly publicized bundled payment initiative has been the "packaging" of heart surgery patients at the Geisinger Health System. This is part of their "ProvenCare" (service mark) Program. This Program involves the identification of best evidence based medical practices for managing patients who have had coronary artery bypass surgery.

The program tracks patients' progress through the emergency room, preoperative and intraoperative care, surgical intensive care unit, monitored bed, regular hospital floor, discharge planning, rehabilitation, and outpatient setting during a 90 day period. [26] *Adelson, A, In Bid for Better Care, Surgery with a Warranty; New York Times; May 17, 2007*

Geisinger Health System (including its inpatient, rehabilitation, and outpatient components, and physicians involved in the care of these patients) receives one fee to cover the costs expended across the care continuum during this 90 day period. In addition, although perhaps stopping short of providing a "warranty", to receive complete reimbursement, certain quality standards must be met.

The Geisinger Health System Coronary Artery Bypass Procedure bundled payment initiative has served as a model for additional methods financed by both the private and public sectors. The most widely reported example has been that launched in the past few years by the federal government. The federal government's Bundled Payment Initiative has had 500 provider participants since 2013, with more on the way.

The federal government's Bundled Payment Initiative is broken into four different models. This initiative is known collectively as the Bundled Payment for Care Initiative (hereafter BPCI). The first of the four models covers the retrospective acute hospital care stay only. Medicare will pay hospitals a discounted amount from that ordinarily paid through the Inpatient Prospective Payment System (IPPS). Physician care in this model will continue to be paid separately for their services under the Medicare Physician Fee Schedule. Under certain circumstances, hospitals and physicians may be able to share gains in this area based upon the results of care redesign.

The second of the four models covers the costs retrospectively of the acute hospital stay, plus post-acute care of Medicare patients. In this model, the episode of care will cover the entire acute hospital stay and all the services delivered during this period, as well as post-acute services for a 30, 60 or 90 day period following hospital discharge. Participants may choose from among 48 clinical conditions to have bundled under this model.

The third of the four models covers retrospectively the costs of post-acute care. In fact, this episode will not be defined and triggered until the end of the acute care stay. The episode will begin with the initiation of services provided through a skilled nursing facility, an inpatient rehabilitation setting, a long term care institution or home care services through an agency. These post-acute services must begin within 30 days of discharge from the hospital and may last up to 30, 60 or 90 days.

As with Model 2, participants in this bundled payment model may choose to have their costs for treating patients from any among 48 different clinical conditions.

Finally, the fourth of the four federal government (Medicare) Bundled Payment models is one in which the hospital will receive a prospectively set payment for the treatment of patients within the acute care setting only. This payment is intended to cover all the costs generated by the hospital, treating physicians and all other practitioners providing services to patients with one of 48 clinical condition episodes.

[27] http://www.innovation.cms.gov/initiatives/bundled-payments/

The focus (to date) on these 500 federal BPCIs occurring across the country has been more on how the payments are to be divided up among the hospital, outpatient facilities and physicians, than of whether all the performance metrics have been met. This was to be expected since at least in those models where one payment needs to be divided up among different institutions and practitioners who are used to receiving their own separate payments, this is quite novel. It has required a period of adjustment, especially for hospitals and physicians.

However, it is in the performance accountability area where there is likely to be the most interesting implications for potential medical liability. Although there is nothing in the language of any of the four models of the BPCI for Medicare patients that would raise the issue of implied warranties, there are expectations for adhering to best evidence based medical practices.

Adherence to these practices serves at least two purposes: One is to be able to deliver sufficiently efficient and economical care (i.e. to minimize the extent of variability of practice among physicians and other practitioners and facilities taking care of patients with specified conditions). However, at the same time, demonstrable adherence to these best practices is also intended to improve the quality of care and patient outcomes, individually and collectively.

Once again, these goals constitute those of the Triple Aim. The big question is whether the final component of the "Quadruple Aim" can be achieved if any of the three goals of achieving the Triple Aim is compromised in the context of the emerging technology driven, post reform healthcare system. Addressing this query will prove to be a recurring theme throughout the rest of this book.

In Chapter 7, we will address how various methods (including the use of advanced information technologies) may be used in the context of these new models for financing and delivering healthcare services to achieve not only the

Triple, but the Quadruple Aim. Before that, we'll explore in Chapters 5 and 6 how to minimize the medical legal risks in the use of various electronic health information technologies.

Chapter 5

How to Use Electronic Health Records to Optimize Care Value and Minimize Medico-Legal Risks

The Early History of Electronic Health Records

Early versions of electronic health records (hereafter EHRs) have been out there for almost a half century. Pioneers such as Drs. William Stead, Octo Barnett, Perry Miller, Lawrence Weed (also the developer of the Problem Oriented Medical Record or POMR) initiated and drove this movement forward from the 1960s to the present day.

Early EHRs, for the most part, were experimental. They were confined largely to the laboratories of these pioneers. They were essentially electronic archiving systems of the clinical information on patients originally handwritten into non-electronic medical records. Nevertheless, in the hands of these pioneers and researchers at their respective academic institutions, they were able to capitalize on having electronic information on patients to facilitate analyses of practice patterns that would have proved elusive in their absence.

A whole community of largely academics grew up in the 1970s and 1980s. They were frequent speakers at the Symposium for Computer Applications in Medical Care (hereafter SCAMC). This yearly get together convened the giants in the field of EHRs. SCAMC was constantly trying to push the envelope of how to use electronic health information technologies to improve the quality, safety and efficiency (i.e. the value) of healthcare delivery.

SCAMC was the 1970s and 1980s Health Care IT geek's version of "Comic-Con". Some of the presentations (which this author attended) consisted of 50 slide PPT presentations comprised entirely of advanced mathematical equations which could be used to analyze large electronic data stores to discern best evidence based medical practices. Another (which the author also attended) was a workshop consisting of Dr. Larry Weed sitting at an early version personal computer. Dr. Weed enthralled at least 50 people (in a seminar room fire codes only intended to hold about 20) getting a peek at his unveiling of his "Knowledge Couplers" methodology. This tool electronically captured and analyzed data to improve clinical decision making and the value of healthcare delivery.

SCAMC continued throughout the 1980s and into the early 1990s (when e-mail and the World Wide Web began to dominate electronically). Large commercial enterprises (such as General Electric, Siemens, McKesson, et. al.) began to poke around in EHRs for the first time. These large companies began to believe that EHRs might be the wave of the future in healthcare (and not just the play toy for academics that they had been for nearly thirty years even by that time).

The ill-fated Clinton Healthcare Reform movement finally brought at least the potential role for the electronic capture and analysis of clinical data as a means to demonstrably and measurably improve the value of healthcare delivery into bold relief. A VBP and Accountable Care precursor brainchild of Dr. Alain Enthoven (Managed Competition), was at the heart of the Clinton Administration's Healthcare Reform efforts. This author corresponded with Dr. Enthoven during this time to dovetail managed competition's goals and metrics with those of VBP. For managed competition to work effectively, providers, payers, purchasers, and patients (the 4Ps) had to come together and agree upon what constituted superior value care and how it could be achieved and demonstrated. This was required so that care could be continuously improved through providing the proper incentives for providers to deliver it, payers and purchasers to recognize and buy it, and patients to receive it. Having EHRs in the context of this managed competition world began to look to some of these large companies (mentioned above) and others as a worthwhile business opportunity.

Clinton's 1300+ page healthcare reform package (largely constructed through a 511 member task force) never really got vetted with Congress, nor very widely, with the "4P's" prior to its unveiling. This author was an advisor to several of the working groups of this mysterious task force (both at a distance and in person). As an example of its clandestine nature, this author was summoned by the Chair of one of the working groups to show up at a pre-designated time in the lobby of the Mayflower Hotel in Washington (a few blocks from the White House). What followed was a three hour interrogation by three members of that working group. This author was instructed not to disclose that this meeting had occurred, nor ever to reveal the names of anybody attending, or what questions were actually asked and answered.

As a result of this largely "cloak and dagger" approach for transforming what was (even 20 years ago) approximately one seventh of the U.S. economy, Clinton's Healthcare Reform initiative imploded when it was finally released to the Congress in 1994. Newt Gingrich (then the Minority Whip in the U.S. House of Representatives) had had plenty of time to embolden his "Contract for America" devotees to mount a fierce counteroffensive. The package was essentially stillborn and never even made it to the floor for a vote of any kind. Despite multiple attempts to revive it, the (huge) baby was smothered in its crib in the summer of 1994. Its defeat turbocharged the Republicans to their blowout takeover of Congress in 1994 (which still impacts the hyper-partisan politics in D.C. to this very day).

Yet, even in the devastating ruins of healthcare reform in 1994, resulting in the postponement of serious discussions of it again for the next 15 years, many seeds had been planted. Perhaps the most important of these ideas involved getting the healthcare payer and purchasing communities (and, the most progressive providers) to begin to evaluate, continuously improve, and demonstrate the superior value of healthcare delivery. They accomplished this through the collection, aggregation, and analysis of electronically generated clinical data. This led to some early demonstration projects in value based purchasing and disease/care management throughout the rest of the 1990s leading up to the landmark work by the Institute of Medicine in November, 1999, "To Err is Human".

The Leapfrog Group's Hospital Grading System and the Patient Safety Movement

If there was ever a report from a body advising the federal government that got people's attention, it was the explosive study by the Institute of Medicine published in November, 1999, better known as "To Err is Human".

[28] Corrigan, K, et al., *To Err is Human: Building a Safer Health System; National Academies Press; Washington, D.C., 2000.*

That study concluded that up to 98,000 Americans died needlessly in hospitals every year as a result of preventable medical errors. That single report jumpstarted the whole patient safety movement across the nation. One of the most notable developments arising from this report was the convening of Fortune 500 CEOs through the Business Roundtable to found the Leapfrog Group in 2000.

The Leapfrog Group (LFG) was formed by 60 Charter members of (largely) Fortune 500 companies who came together and agreed to evaluate hospitals and health systems (initially) on three measures determined to be associated with delivering superior value care. These three measures were:

- Whether they had implemented computerized physician order entry (hereafter CPOE) systems (often embedded in EHR systems);
- Whether they had full time intensivists (physicians board certified or eligible in Critical Care Medicine) covering their intensive care units (although some time later remote coverage through an electronic ICU or e-ICU was permitted to fulfill this measure); and
- Whether they were only doing a list of invasive procedures for which they could document that they performed a sufficient number of them annually to be able to demonstrate optimal clinical outcomes. If they did not perform this requisite number of procedures annually, they would need to be able to demonstrate that the outcomes of their patients were at least as good as they were in those hospitals that did perform a benchmark number of procedures.

Over the years, working with the National Quality Forum (hereafter NQF), the LFG added about 30 additional quality measures to evaluate hospitals and health systems. Using all these quality measures, the LFG through various surveys and other means now evaluates and ranks participating hospitals through a letter grading system, utilizing “A”, “B”, “C”, “D” and “F” performance marks.

For probably the first 10 years of its existence, the LFG did not gain a whole lot of traction as far as being an influential force in healthcare. However, during the past few years (especially since the passage of the ACA in March, 2010), the letter grading system has gained much more notoriety and influence. This has certainly been the case when prestigious hospitals (usually academic medical centers) ranking highest annually in the highly quoted “U.S. News & World Report” have not been awarded terribly high letter grades by the LFG.

Of course, whenever another round of Leapfrog letter grades is published, there is the ever predictable complaint of these hospitals and health systems who obtain a grade of "C" or below. The usual justifications coming from these prestigious (largely academic) medical institutions is that the Leapfrog Group has not sufficiently taken into account the average severity of illness of their patients, when doing their evaluations. They say that they are the "hospitals of last resort". They (as tertiary and quaternary institutions) get the sickest patients that other hospitals can't manage and pass onto them. Consequently, their patients' outcomes are necessarily worse (all other factors remaining equal) than those of more community-based institutions. They also add that the data upon which their Leapfrog Grade is based are outdated, and that they have addressed any problems and "are much better now" than when Leapfrog evaluated them.

However, much of the Leapfrog Group's evaluations still are based on hospitals and health systems' having certain structures and processes such as CPOE, intensivists in ICUs, and adherence to best evidence based medical practices in place, as opposed to strictly outcome-based assessments. So, if anything, the large academic institutions should have an advantage over community-based hospitals. They have greater access to the financial, technological and human resources required to implement and use CPOE, to provide for intensivists in their ICUs or to have access to e-ICU technologies, and to deliver sufficient volume, best evidence based practices leading to superior patient outcomes.

It is fair to speculate that in the not too distant future (if not already), evidence of a defendant hospital's or health system's Leapfrog Group grade for a particular year in which it was evaluated (when an allegedly negligent act had resulted in patient injury) may be admissible into evidence. Of course, to overcome even initial admissibility objections, plaintiffs' attorneys would need to show that a hospital or health system's Leapfrog Group grade was both relevant and connected to a particular case of alleged negligence, when it occurred.

There would have to be some preliminary demonstration that at the time of the allegedly negligent act (or omission) the hospital did not have in place (or performed relatively poorly) on one of more of the Leapfrog Group measures. To go further and prove that this may have constituted a negligently committed (or omitted) action resulting in recoverable damages, such an act or omission would have to be a direct and proximate cause of the patient's injury. Perhaps, it could be that the CPOE system either was not installed, not functioning effectively, and/or not used properly by defendant physicians or other providers receiving and implementing orders from this system. If the hospital or health system got dinged for this in its Leapfrog Group evaluation, then there could be some grounds (at least on the basis of relevance and timeliness) for admitting this finding into evidence.

However, plaintiffs would need to overcome the strong public policy argument for not admitting into evidence quality or safety improvement measures. For this argument to hold water, defendants would have to be able to make the case that the primary purpose of the Leapfrog Group rating system is to improve care, not to simply evaluate it to assist employers, insurers, unions and patients to become more informed value-based purchasers. This latter purpose was, after all, a prime, if not *the* prime, original motivating purpose for the Fortune 500 CEO members of the Business Roundtable for founding and chartering the Leapfrog Group back in 2000. However, there could be a strong argument made these days that the primary purpose of the Leapfrog Group is to improve the quality, safety, and efficiency (i.e. the value) of care for everybody (not just to facilitate VBP to benefit purchasers).

As stated earlier, the Leapfrog Group did not really gain sufficient traction to become as influential with its grading system as what it has now become until the ACA was passed in March, 2010. However, more than a year prior to the ACA's passage, was the enactment of the HITECH portion of the Stimulus Law (signed by President Obama on February 17, 2009, less than a month into his presidency). It is this legislation which provides for over $30 billion for hospitals and physicians to demonstrate their "meaningful use" of EHRs that has had an even greater impact than Leapfrog and its requirement for CPOE (and other measures) on the growth and development of electronic health information technologies. The impact of the HITECH act and its patient safety/risk management implications follow in the next section below.

The HITECH (Health Information Technology Economic and Clinical Health) Act—Demonstrating the Meaningful Use of EHRs

During President Obama's first month in office, the global economy and stock markets were in free fall and the financial system had frozen. With the support of the Federal Reserve and the top officials of his Administration, he drove through Congress what has become known as the Stimulus Law. The Stimulus Law (more officially known as the American Recovery and

Reinvestment Act of 2009, hereafter ARRA) increased spending by about $805 billion through the end of September, 2013, according to the nonpartisan Congressional Budget Office (hereafter CBO). Although still very controversial to this day, the CBO has since estimated that this spending added substantially to economic growth which would not likely have occurred in its absence. ARRA also decreased the poverty rate, while adding less than 0.1% to the nation's long term debt burden. This calculation accounted for how much would need to have been borrowed anyhow, over the next 75 years to fund the Social Security, Medicare and Medicaid Programs.

Within that $805 billion of new spending was allocated somewhere around $30 billion to support the "meaningful use" of EHRs. This hefty chunk of change came courtesy of the HITECH portion of the ARRA. Within HITECH is an extensive legislative litany of all the goals for improving the quality, safety, efficiency and value of healthcare delivery that this level of investment in EHRs should be able to help achieve. This, of course, assumes that EHRs *are meaningfully used (as defined and as have been further specified through extensive subsequent regulations) by hospitals and other eligible providers.*

By the end of June, 2014, over $24 billion had already been expended on behalf of both hospitals and "eligible providers" (i.e. physicians and other named types of practitioners) to promote their meaningful use of EHRs. Depending on whether they qualify through the Medicare or Medicaid program, physicians (and other eligible providers) may be subsidized to the extent of $44,000 to $58,000, respectively. However, to obtain these subsidies, they must be able attest to (and later demonstrate) their meaningful use of EHRs as established by Stage 1, 2 and 3 requirements. Hospitals, depending on their size and geographic location (including the economic and demographic characteristics of their patients and surrounding communities) could collect between $2 and $10 million (approximately although the amounts vary according to a host of factors) for their demonstrated meaningful use of EHRs.

However, by the middle of 2014, even Stage 2 meaningful use requirements are considered by most providers (especially physicians) to be too difficult for them to satisfy. Multiple extensions and allowances for further delay in meeting these new requirements have already been given, so much so that now Stage 3 requirements will not be enforceable before 2017.

A more extensive analysis of the HITECH portion of the Stimulus Law (and all the requirements for meaningfully using EHRs under Stage 1, 2 and 3 requirements) is beyond the scope of this book. Such analyses can be found through many sources, including those found at:

[29] http://www.healthit.gov.

For purposes of this book, the overriding goal of HITECH has always been to incent providers to use EHRs in such a way as to optimize their chances for achieving the Triple Aim. However, the underlying question remains whether the Triple Aim can be accomplished, without also achieving the fourth component of the Quadruple Aim, i.e. decreasing the likelihood and actuality of medical liability actions. Failure to achieve the Quadruple Aim will make accomplishment of the Triple Aim a hollow victory.

How to Use Electronic Health Records to Achieve the Quadruple Aim

Electronic Health Records (EHRs) may well represent the single biggest change in the practice of medicine and the delivery of health care since the "germ theory" of disease. Such a change is absolutely essential to begin to remove the trillion dollars per year of medical waste that is bankrupting the country and its citizens, and placing the U.S. at a competitive disadvantage in the global marketplace.

But what are some of the pitfalls (that need to be identified and avoided) in implementing EHRs in an effort to achieve the Triple (and hopefully the Quadruple) Aim? Princeton Insurance Company analyzed closed and open medical liability claims over a six year period. Princeton Insurance used the Harvard Risk Management tool to identify the most frequent fundamental contributors to these medical liability claims. Through use of a comprehensive coding manual and trained Princeton abstractors, the Harvard tool permitted a detailed analysis of these medical liability claims filed against Princeton Insurance physician and hospital policyholders over a six year period.

[8] *Princeton Insurance. Electronic medical records: Patient Safety and Risk Management Guide. Princeton Insurance; 2009.*

http://www.pinsco.com/downloads/EMRUsersGuide_final.pdf.

The results of the analysis showed that failure of clinical judgment was a contributing factor in 86% of all claims. Inadequate communication (either between physicians and their patients and families or between and among treating providers) was a factor in 47% of claims. Insufficient and/or inaccurate communication contributed to 30% of claims and suboptimal office systems (to be defined better below) was a factor in 18% of claims. These were the top four contributors to these medical liability claims. Their incidences add up to more than 100%, because it was usually the case that medical liability claims had more than one key contributing factor.

[8] *Cf. Princeton Insurance; p. 1.*

These are the four broad areas (clinical judgment, communication, documentation, and office systems) for which the appropriate use of EHRs can and should have the greatest beneficial impact in minimizing the incidence, magnitude and success of the significant majority of medical liability claims. However, this is a double edged sword. If the various functionalities of EHRs intended to improve the quality and safety of healthcare delivery are not installed, not used, ignored, or misused, then there may be whole new avenues of medical liability potential open up. Some of these pitfalls are discussed below:

Medical Legal Pitfalls Associated with the Use of Electronic Health Records

Pitfalls in Using EHRs to Communicate with Patients and Their Families

EHRs may facilitate communications between physicians and other providers and their patients and families, including printed clinical summaries from office visits and discharge instructions following hospitalizations. Some EHR systems allow automatic download of the above information to a patient's own electronic personal health record (hereafter PHR). Some electronic PHRs may also automatically upload this new information into their provider's EHR on them. Finally, many leading electronic record systems permit automatic translation of follow up instructions in the patient's native tongue.

[8] *Cf. Princeton Insurance at 14, 16.*

However, there are at least two major medical legal pitfalls that need to be overcome:

- *"Reducing patient communications for fear of disclosure:* Moving to an electronic records environment may create anxieties in patients concerning the security, confidentiality and privacy of their personal health information. Patients and their families may not be as open in their communications with physicians and other caregivers as in the past non-electronic environment. To overcome this, physicians must explain the security feature their EHRs possess to ensure the continuing privacy and confidentiality of their personal medical information.

- *Alienating Patients:* Physicians could alienate patients by taking too much time typing and not enough time talking with patients. This is particularly troublesome when facing away from the patient because of the design of the room. Physicians should consider having nurse managers or other staff members in the room to record the information while the physician talks with the patient, at least for the initial stages of implementation."

  [8] *Cf. Princeton at 17.*

Pitfalls in Using EHRs to Communicate between and Among other Providers

Some of these EHR features to improve communication among providers within the same practice or office could include:

- *"Improving intra-practice communications.* This enhanced communication may be achieved via electronic messaging or texting, transmission of clinical task of "to do" lists (including alerts and reminders) or electronic capture and communication of telephone messages.
- *Reminders* for appointment scheduling, missed appointment alerts, ordering of labs and consults, and perhaps e-mail communications to reduce handoff communication errors, while enhancing productivity.
- *Checklists Within and Across Offices of a Practice* that enhance clarity through legibility and consistent presentation can go a long way to preventing miscommunication."

  [8] Cf. Princeton Insurance, generally, from pp. 5-9

However, suboptimal or misguided communications could increase liability potential by:

- *"Closing tasks without requiring action.* Never close a task without taking some kind of action on it, or explaining why nothing was done.

- *Relying too much on electronic communications.* This can degrade intra-office communications. Maintain ongoing face-to-face communications.
- *Not requiring ALL office providers to use the EHR."*
  [8] *Cf. Princeton at 10.*

Pitfalls in Using EHRs to Communicate Among Providers Outside of the Practice

Full interoperability involves the ability to share all the electronically ggregated information on a patient in real time with others (including those at e point of care). *Partial Interoperability* only permits this degree of sharing ith those on compatible electronic systems. This may also be referred to in e some contexts as *substituted interoperability*.

Either type of interoperable record (but especially those that are only rtially interoperable) may result in:

- *"The Creation of Useless Electronically Generated Consultation Request* with uninterpretable checklists or other material or because of too much information that confuses the consultant. Use free text where clarity is required, and more focused box checking.
- *Failure to Use Available Interoperability.* Physicians and other who have the capabilities to transmit or receive information electronically or through interoperable systems, but who do not do so, could find themselves in a difficult defensive posture. Physicians should use whatever capabilities they have at their disposal in their EHR systems to transmit all relevant electronic (as well as non-electronic) information as part of all of their patients' medical records."

[8] *Cf. Princeton at generally at pp.10-12.*

To paraphrase from the first "Spiderman" movie: "With great power, nes great responsibility". That is an important admonition for those using ctronic health records.

EHRs do confer great powers to communicate with patients, their families, other providers and healthcare personnel within and outside a medical ctice concerning the conditions of patients and how to improve their care. wever, physicians (and others involved in the care delivery process) may to take advantage of these newfound capabilities for communicating ely, accurate and complete information to other providers in real time and at the point of care. If that capability does exist, and physicians don't take advantage of it to communicate to patients and their families concerning how to facilitate their own informed and improved clinical decision making, this may result in new liability exposure in the event of suboptimal clinical outcomes.

The next section will focus on the accuracy and sufficiency of the EHR content itself, how it is transmitted and used to improve patient care management.

Pitfalls in the Content, Accuracy, Sufficiency and Mechanics of EHRs

The *content* of medical records (whether handwritten or electronic) pertains to the actual substance of the information captured and sought to be communicated. This information concerns the patient's chief complaint, history of present illness, symptoms, signs, syndromes, clinical lab, pathology and imaging study results, along with current working diagnoses. The content also includes completed, ongoing or proposed treatments, consultation summaries, and the patient's ongoing progress (or lack thereof), among other things.

The *accuracy* of medical records (whether handwritten or electronic) concerns whether the content of clinical information (as summarized above) and other information (e.g. demographics, etc.) reflects reality at the time that it was entered into the record. Here is where electronically entered information (and the metadata which may indicate exactly when information was reported, recorded and acted upon) can be a godsend for ensuring the accuracy of medical records and the treatments which follow.

"Of course, failure to take advantage of this capability (i.e. the metadata indicating the precise time that information became available, when it was recorded and by whom, and the actions that were taken or not taken subsequently) can be a double edged sword. Because of the quite liberal rules of discovery applicable in medical liability cases, this metadata may well be discoverable in civil litigation. Should the metadata exist and it shows that not having taken the precise timing of critical information about a patient's condition into account at the time a treatment was administered, that could substantially raise the risk of medical liability. Also, electronically retrievable information may make it substantially easier and much quicker for the plaintiff's attorney to collect and present everything necessary to make out a case of liability. 'Electronic foot printing' records entries by whom and when (i.e. the 'metadata' or 'data about data'"

[30] Korin JB, Quattrone MS. Electronic Health Records Raise New Risks of Malpractice Liability. NJLJ [Internet]. 2007 Jun 19;CLXXXVIII(11 – INDEX 893). - See more at:

http://www.lawtechnologynews.com/id=900005483988/Electronic-Health-Records-Raise-New-Risks-of-Malpractice-Liability.

The *sufficiency* of medical records (whether handwritten or electronic) has to do with whether the information recorded is complete for purposes of describing a patient's condition and its progress, tests results, response to various treatments (or lack thereof) and further medical management plans (if any)…Having access to electronically captured information about patients ensures a greater likelihood of obtaining complete information on patients at the point of care. This should optimize informed clinical decision making (assuming that such information is accessible across interoperable EHR systems).

"EHRs may improve the sufficiency of medical record information (and therefore its content and accuracy or clarity) through the use of checklists and templates, compilation of both electronic and non-electronic sources of patient information, and straddling both mechanics and sufficiency…"

[8] *Cf. Princeton Insurance at 21.*

These checklists and templates can be very helpful to ensure obtaining complete information about patients. "Assisting in the creation of a robust medical record, EHRs come with abundant checklists and vendor or user-customizable templates to ensure that all questions are asked, body systems checked, and relevant test, procedures, diagnostic and therapeutic interventions are at least considered. These electronic screens may then present the information produced in a particular order, with graphical displays of patients' clinical results over time correlated with specific therapies, or in tandem with consultation, laboratory and/or radiological findings. This virtually eliminates the tedious and error prone process of hunting for the clinical highlights from the patient's previous visits. In addition, information and clinical findings from checklists generated during prior office visits, including those previously checked 'within normal limits' (WNL) may be easily viewed for comparative purposes."

[8] *Cf. Princeton Insurance at 22-3.*

Finally, there are the *mechanics* of medical record keeping. EHRs may eliminate problems with illegibility or incorrect methods to correct medical records. This may cast doubt on the credibility of any physician irrespective of the quality of care actually delivered.

"With all the leading EHR systems, once the EHR is locked, any alteration must be in the form of a formal 'addendum'. Some leading ambulatory systems label any alteration to the EHR as an 'addendum' even if made before the physician or other provider user formally signs off on the record and 'locks' it. In addition, EHRs may be used to:

- Eliminate confusing abbreviations and acronyms;
- Differentiate among similarly spelled (or pronounced) medications;
- Eliminate preceding and trailing '0s' for order and prescriptions (which may result in substantial, even lethal, dosing);
- Auto-date and precisely time entries; and
- Ensure any alterations to a completed record are done appropriately."

[8] *Cf. Princeton at 18-19.*

Despite all the obvious advantages of being able to use EHRs to ensure the accurate, complete and timely content of information, the following represents a list of potential pitfalls which could increase liability potential should physicians and other providers not use these capabilities fully and appropriately:

- *"Use of multiple physician templates* causing confusion, missed facts, poor assumptions, and less than optimal decision making;
- *Having a nurse complete a portion of the medical record history and physician and having that be inconsistent with the physician record:*
- *The loss of critical patient information within an office by "unchecking" boxes (without explaining in free text why this was done)*
- *Overuse of checkboxes without using* free text option to supplement check off generated history and physician reports.
- *Auto-population of symptoms and findings for "standard" illnesses* once some subset of those is entered should be avoided.
- *Alteration of EHRs:* The time-honored way of altering handwritten medical records (i.e. crossing out information to be changed with one horizontal line, identifying added information with date, time, and signature) should be sought and used appropriately whenever seeking to alter EHRs.
- *Importation of medical journal articles:* Physicians should never incorporate such articles into patient EMRs until and unless they have

thoroughly researched all the literature and have included all relevant literature, explaining their course of action.

- *Not understanding the extent of interoperability*: The danger lies in assuming that a particular EHR system is more interoperable than it is, leading to assumptions and actions that may negatively impact care because of a missing (non-communicated) piece of critical information.
- *EHRs staying open 'too long':* Such a feature to permit the incorporation of late breaking lab, X-ray or procedural results may be a liability risk unless there is in an auditable manner concerning who alters the medical record, and in what ways, during this period that the record remains 'open'."

  [8] *Cf. Princeton Insurance at 24, 26-7.*

Despite these potential pitfalls, one of the biggest obstacles that has stood in the path of optimal medical care for millennia has been not being able to obtain quickly in real time at the point of care complete, accurate and timely clinical and other important information on patients. EHRs (which may meet the current and future requirements for interoperability) for the first time have brought that "brass ring" of clinical quality within reach. That fact alone makes them well worth it.

The Proper Use of Office and Clinical Systems

"EHRs offer various types of alerts for physicians and office staff to utilize for follow up on patients to ensure that they are adhering to instructions, receiving prescribed medications, undertaking recommended tests and interventions, and making or keeping critical follow up appointments. Some of these alerts to prevent patients from being lost to follow up include:

- *Missed Appointment Alerts;*
- *Alerts for Failure to Obtain Prescribed Medications:*
- *Alerts for Past Due Tests or Consultation Results; and*
- *Alerts for Laboratory Panic Values"*

[8] *Cf. Princeton Insurance at 28-29.*

Screening and Preventive Health Reminders

"Screening tests recommendations are embedded into most of the leading ambulatory EHR products. They include (among other things) preventive health screenings most appropriate based on a patient's age, gender, health status, and other factors. EHR clinical systems may contain preventive health templates which keep track of all the screening tests that have been completed on patients as well as when the next ones will be due, such as:

- All types of cancer screenings (e.g. breast, cervical, prostate, colorectal);
- Cholesterol (all types) and triglyceride screening, blood sugar screening (including glucose tolerance tests);
- Blood pressure monitoring;
- Bone densitometry for post-menopausal women;
- All vaccinations for children (including chickenpox and meningitis), pneumonia and influenza vaccines for children, those over 50 and healthcare workers; and
- Hepatitis vaccines for healthcare workers."
  [8] Cf. Princeton at 32.

These reminders may also prevent future claims of neglect should failure to do these ever result in adverse outcomes which become the subject of litigation. However, the following potential pitfalls need to be recognized and avoided:

- *"Alert or Reminder Fatigue:* The challenge for physicians is how to set the thresholds to screen out enough of these alerts and reminders to maintain clinical process workflow without risking missing something which could make a positive difference in their patients' care…
- *Ignoring or Overriding Drug Safety or Laboratory Results Alerts:* By setting drug safety or laboratory results alerts at a threshold where they trigger too readily, physicians may be held accountable for following up on the suggestions deriving from these alerts. They may need to justify when they chose to override or ignore those alerts which either didn't make sense, or which could have been disregarded

due to unique patient care factors, or where the benefits of changing course were dubious…" [8] Cf. Princeton generally at 34

"The best advice is to have clearly documented your justification for setting the thresholds where you did. You would need also to be able to state why in your best clinical judgment you were comfortable in not responding to alerts based on the patient's unique characteristics and overriding need for specific types of therapies."

[8] *Cf. Princeton at 34.*

All of the above pitfalls, admittedly, derive from the capabilities in EHRs that have been added to help users meet the Triple Aim. However, failure to install them, set alert thresholds at justifiable levels, heed and act upon them on a timely basis may result in even greater liability than if those capabilities were not present.

The potential benefits and pitfalls of the improved diagnostic and therapeutic decision making capabilities of EHRs to facilitate good clinical judgment, the lack of which may be the most frequent causes of medical liability, follow in the concluding section of this chapter below.

Clinical Judgment: Optimizing Decision Making Aids While Avoiding Medical Legal Pitfalls

"Gaps in clinical judgment (including both diagnostic and therapeutic decision making) were implicated in more of the medical liability claims in the Princeton Insurance study than any other (85%). Within these 85% of claims, 86% involved patient assessment issues, 37% failures or delays in obtaining appropriate consultations or referrals to facilitate better diagnostic and/or therapeutic decision making, 34% having to do with the selection and management of the therapy, itself, and 20% dealing with patient monitoring."

[8] *Cf. Princeton Insurance, generally, at 35*

- *Differential Diagnosis Generation.* "These systems are found in a few of the leading ambulatory EHR systems. They have been around as research and educational tools for decades. When turned on, they can produce for physicians various differential diagnoses to consider (and rule in or rule out). Based on the input of certain historical, clinical and pathologic (laboratory and X-ray/imaging) findings. Some of the more recent systems have been shown to suggest the final diagnosis in 95 to 98% of real cases in multi-center clinical studies."

[15] *Isabel: A Web-Based Differential Diagnostic Aid for Pediatrics—Results from an Initial Performance Evaluation. Archives of Diseases of Childhood; May, 2003.*

"Radiology/imaging differential diagnostic systems embedded in a few of the leading EHR systems may even suggest which studies may improve the physician's pre-to post-test probability of a suspected diagnosis to the greatest extent. These embedded radiology information systems (RIS) may also caution against use of certain procedures based on a patient's condition and known hypersensitivities (e.g. to certain radiographic dyes). They may even caution against certain studies due to their radiation dosage (where's a patient's cumulative lifetime dosage may be downloadable from his EHR or personal health record, PHR)."

[8] *Cf. Princeton Insurance generally at 37.*

"The benefits of the use of these systems should be weighed heavily against the ability to respond to all of the differential diagnoses provided. Similar to alerts, not responding can create a difficult defense should a suggested possible diagnosis, that was not considered turn out to be the actual diagnosis. At the very least, physicians should be prepared to state in the EHR why they did not believe that the alternatives suggested should be considered." [8] *Cf. Princeton at 37-8*

Therapeutic Decision Making

"These therapeutic decision making aides may include:

- *Best Practice Guidelines (by Specialty and/or Condition):* These may derive from those developed and promulgated from various national medical specialty societies or from www.guideline.gov (which serves as a governmental repository of guidelines).
- *Medication Prescribing Alerts:* Leading EHR products have medication error prevention functionalities such as those to avoid:
  - *Drug-Drug Interactions*;
  - *Drug-Food Interactions*;

- *Drug Overdosing/Under-dosing:* These could be due to such factors as patient age, body size, kidney function, or even (calculated) drug distribution and absorption rates;
- *Drug Allergies*;
- *Contraindicated Drugs:* Color-coded as either relatively, or absolutely, contraindicated; and
- *Drug/Laboratory Value Precautions and 'Panic Value' Alerts:* These would be triggered if a patient is prescribed a medication which could further aggravate a metabolic condition reflected by worsening laboratory results."

[8] *Cf. Princeton Insurance generally at 40 and 42.*

- Health and Disease Management Templates:

  "EHRs include health maintenance and disease management templates that facilitate appropriate care for patients with similar conditions or characteristics, such as sex and age. Guidelines are provided for active searching, and signal alerts for any patients not meeting these guidelines—the benefits of which are in preventing certain missed diagnoses, resulting in failure to treat allegations."

  [8] *Cf. Princeton Insurance at 43*

  Despite the obvious benefits of using these various therapeutic decision making capabilities embedded in EHRs, there are various liability pitfalls that need to be avoided. These include (but may not be limited to):

  - "Not documenting the rationale for not heeding best practice or health/disease management guidelines; and/or
  - Blindly adhering to best practice guidelines: Physicians (and others) should not blindly adhere to best evidence based guidelines without taking into account individual body size, co-morbidities, kidney function, and a myriad of other clinical and non-clinical factors impacting therapeutic choices (including, increasingly in the future, each patient's genetic profile)."

[8] *Cf. Princeton Insurance, generally, at 44.*

Process and Outcomes Tracking and Management

"To the extent that information can be stored in an electronic database, these EHR products may well be able to track physicians' performance and their patients' clinical outcomes in some or all of the following ways:

- *Tracking of physicians' following of best practice guidelines:* Many of the leading EHR systems can keep track of their physician users' percentage adherence with best practice guidelines and disease/health management protocols. These systems may benchmark physician EHR user adherence relative to that of other physician EHR users of the same system regionally and nationally. Physician users need to ensure that their lack of adherence with best practice guidelines or health/disease management protocols is not counted against them if they document justifiable reasons for not adhering.
- *Tracking of the rate of physicians' recommending to patients screening and preventive health maintenance interventions when due:* Similarly, most of the leading EHR systems can also track the rate of physician EHR users' recommending of the screening and preventive health maintenance guidelines to their patients (when it is timely and appropriate for them to do so)…
- *Tracking Patients' Outcomes:* Physicians and their patients (either through their EHRs or PHRs, respectively) may track and evaluate their outcomes longitudinally over time in response to various treatment regimens. This may help both physicians and their patients to independently and jointly manage care and track treatment results more effectively. However, this feature may be used not only as a shield by physicians, but as a sword by plaintiffs' attorneys and their medical experts, to the extent that such outcomes tracking is discoverable in litigation" *[8] Cf. Princeton Insurance at 45.*

Potential Pitfalls of the Physician Performance Measurement and Tracking Feature

This feature could be quite valuable to physicians (and others seeking to evaluate and continuously improve their performance). However, if not properly used, it could result in potential medical legal pitfalls, such as:

"--*Potential Discovery of the Tracking of Physician Performance:* This could pose a potential pitfall for physicians using EHRs with this functionality. Some leading ambulatory (and hospital) EHRs may track and compile statistically robust analyses concerning the percentage adherence of their physician users with various best practices suggested by the EHR software for particular types of patients. However, the downside of this would be if this were discoverable by plaintiffs' attorneys. They and their experts could seek to demonstrate the relative non-adherence of a defendant physician user of this EHR software with the types of best practices which (arguably had they been followed) could have prevented a patient's injury. *To address this pitfall, physician users must first be aware that this capability exists and that their EHRs may be using it. Next, physicians must ensure that whenever they don't follow best practice guidelines or disease/health management protocols, they document why they are not adhering. Such justified non-adherence then should not be held against physicians in compiling their performance profiles."[8] Cf. Princeton Insurance at 46*

"--*Potential Discovery of Patients' Outcomes:* Patients' clinical outcomes may be tracked over time (through a longitudinal Continuity of Care capability). Physicians (or other clinicians in their office) should periodically review these patients' electronic records. In doing so, they should ensure that these records do not reveal worrisome trends in patient outcomes, (as measured by lab results, progressive X-ray changes and other parameters in response to treatment, or lack of treatment) that could provide evidence of neglect to potential plaintiffs' attorneys and/or their medical experts."

[8] *Cf. Princeton Insurance at 46.*

EHRs carry great potential for benefits toward achieving the "Triple Aim" of improving health care, health and efficiencies. However, without their proper use, there is a real risk of new and expanded medical liability. The over $30 billion in taxpayer money subsidizing providers' "meaningful use" of EHRs will make it even more incumbent them to use the quality and safety improvement functionalities in EHR systems appropriately. Otherwise, they may well subject themselves to even greater medical legal scrutiny for their failure to achieve the "Triple Aim", let alone the "Quadruple Aim". An analysis of the medical legal risk implications deriving from the use of other advanced electronic health information technologies (beyond EHRs) to help providers achieve the Quadruple Aim follows in Chapter 6 immediately below.

Chapter 6

Medical Liability Risk Implications of Analytics Technologies and Methodologies

Predictive Modeling Technologies

Actuaries have been using predictive modeling systems for quite a while now. The actuaries' main job is to be able to predict based on an insured population's size, demographic mix (age, gender, geographic location, socioeconomics, etc.) and past healthcare utilization history what the future medical costs of that population are likely to be. After making those predictions, actuaries then "rate" that covered population. Doing that assists underwriters in coming up with policies to cover individual members of that population for sets of services for particular periods of time at specific premium levels per month. Policies set by underwriters may be subject to certain exclusions and other adjustments (where legally permissible to do so, especially now following passage of the ACA which outlawed many previously used exclusions).

Predictive modeling (by whatever name it was called) began to find a place in the clinical world only about 25 to 30 years ago. Some severity indexing companies, like MediQual Systems, Inc. (now part of Cardinal Health), of Westborough, MA could claim that they were applying clinical prediction models as far back as the 1980s. The employer-dominated, Pennsylvania Healthcare Cost Containment Council (PHC4), in May, 1987, mandated that all 307 Pennsylvania Hospitals implement the MediGroups software system of MediQual Systems. This system was designed to provide a uniform yardstick for measuring the relative severity of illness-adjusted clinical outcomes and cost effectiveness of these hospitals. Accomplishing this was intended to facilitate an early form of value based purchasing by employers and insurance companies.

The MedisGroups software algorithms could determine the relative pretreatment severity of illness of patients presenting for treatment at these hospitals. The software accomplished this by interfacing with key clinical findings, KCFs, and other demographic data obtained directly from patients' medical records. Based on pretreatment severity of illness calculated in this way, the software could predict (with a high degree of statistical validity when the sample size got to be large enough) what patients' post-treatment clinical outcomes should be. Within similar severity groupings, then, these patients' post-treatment illness severities could be "observed", and compared to what was predicted ("expected").

Observed post-treatment outcomes could be measured as being one, two or even three standard deviations better or worse than what had been predicted based on patients' pretreatment severity of illness. These analyses and results were depicted in numerous graphical displays that were made available to employers and other healthcare purchasers, including the public.

The PHC4, despite several near death experiences, has continued to publish hospital and physician performance data to the present day. It now publishes data regularly on observed vs. expected, severity of illness-adjusted clinical and financial results on 16 medical and surgical conditions at the 157 hospitals and health systems that remain in Pennsylvania. The PHC4 also publishes data on readmissions. Readmissions have become increasingly important for hospitals to measure and minimize to avoid being classified as "outliers" with increasing Medicare reimbursement penalties. All this has continued to put Pennsylvania at the forefront of the transparency and value based purchasing movements now sweeping the country in the wake of national healthcare reform.

Beyond those programs used by the PHC4, other software programs have made significant inroads into clinical predictive modeling. Companies such as Active Health Management (now part of the Healthagen subsidiary of Aetna) and Anvita Health (now part of Humana), have been pioneers in this effort. These companies have access to large clinical data stores and the software algorithms necessary to predict with a significant degree of accuracy and reliability the projected outcomes and costs for treating various populations of patients. This will be an indispensable capability for any hospital, health system, or medical group either as part of or separate from accountable care organizations (ACOs). These ACOs will need these capabilities to be able to take on clinical and financial risk (either with or without payers) as healthcare reform continues to transform the delivery and financing system for the rest of this decade and beyond.

MEDICAL LEGAL IMPLICATIONS OF PREDICTIVE MODELING SYSTEMS

What are the medical legal implications of clinical predictive modeling? Can (or should) providers be expected to use them to allocate their clinical, technological, and financial resources to achieve the greatest improvements in the health status of their patients per dollar invested? If they use these systems, and their results fall significantly short (either in the care of entire populations, some segments of them, or even specific individuals), should these findings even be admissible into evidence in a medical liability case?

We are probably still a few years away from seeing clinical predictive modeling systems admitted into evidence by plaintiffs or defendants to strengthen or weaken, respectively, liability claims. However, there *could (even now)* be a case of *corporate or enterprise* liability argued against a hospital, health system, or even a large medical group, whose clinical results fell significantly below severity of illness adjusted expectations. This could be the case if clinical outcomes for a clinical enterprise could be shown to be consistently two or three standard deviations below what would be expected given the average pretreatment illness severity of their patients. Of course, to recover, an individual plaintiff would still have to prove all the other elements of liability discussed in Chapter 3 by the preponderance of the evidence, resulting in compensable injury.

Corporate liability cases have been around now for about a half century. The "Darling" case got the whole movement started, although it has evolved considerably since then.

[31] *"Darling vs. Charleston Community Memorial Hospital" at 31 Ill. 2d 326 Sept. 29, 1965).*

The legal theory of corporate liability derives from the failure of a hospital (but it could be a health system or even a large medical group) to adequately "patrol its ranks". Every clinical enterprise needs to have in place adequate quality management, peer review, medical credentialing and other means to protect its patients from negligently inflicted harm. Healthcare is becoming increasingly transparent. These clinical prediction systems are more prevalent, accurate and reliable. Clinical enterprises of all sizes and types will need to keep the capabilities of these systems in mind to minimize the risks of corporate (or enterprise) liability claims.

POPULATION HEALTH MANAGEMENT (PHM)

For millennia, the fundamental healthcare transaction has been between one physician and one patient (at least at any one point in time). However, then came increasing specialization and sub-specialization in medicine, especially during the second half of the twentieth century to the present day. So, one patient might very well have a network of physicians working to try to maintain or restore his or her health. Yet, still, the basic transaction (as physicians are always eager to emphasize) remained as that between one physician and one patient.

In the 21st Century, healthcare is transforming from a severely fragmented, disjointed, often chaotic (for the patient and his family) $3 trillion cottage industry into a more integrated system. This new system is focused on improving the health of designated populations for whose clinical and financial results groups of providers have become accountable. There still is the one-on-one relationship between a patient and his or her physician (or physician's assistant, advanced nurse practitioner, nurse midwife, physician extender, or, perhaps, soon, medical robot). Nevertheless, physicians need to take into account in their medical decisions not just the immediate needs of the patients in front of them, but also those of all others in the population(s) for whose results they will be held clinically and financially accountable. They need to be concerned about the 99.9% of patients that aren't in front of them at any given time, as well as the 99.9% of the time that the patients currently in front of them are not in front of them.

Medical students and resident physicians, at least prior to the Prospective Payment System, were taught to spare no expense in saving the lives of patients. As just one example, this could (and did) mean in this author's personal and professional experience draining the existing local blood bank reserve to try to save the life of one patient. This patient had virtually no chance of survival due to hemorrhaging esophageal varices resulting from 50 years of alcoholism. Young accident victims coming into the Emergency Department had to be re-routed due to lack of readily available blood.

This represented a ridiculous case of putting the perceived needs of the one above the real needs of the many, reminiscent of a Captain Kirk vs. Mr. Spock philosophy in the third Star Trek movie, "In Search of Spock" (1984). This process and result would never be tolerated in the second decade of the 21st century because of the huge corporate liability risk to the hospital, if for no other reason. Moreover, in a post-reform world, there are many other compelling reasons (beyond that of avoiding corporate liability). There is a premium on effective and efficient clinical resource utilization to optimize population health management. This has to be the case in all types of situations for which the judicious use of limited resources could really make a positive and measurable difference in the health of the overall population.

That is what population health is (or should be). The focus has to be on how to utilize limited prospectively allocated resources (financial, technological, and human) in the most cost effective manner. The goal needs to be achievement of the greatest measurable, documentable improvements in the collective health of designated populations of patients per dollar invested. Being able to do this will produce the predictability in future healthcare costs which both private and public sector purchasers of healthcare will increasingly demand. Those integrated provider systems which can accomplish this, and thereby continue to win healthcare delivery contracts from private and public sector purchasers will survive and thrive. Those who can't will do neither.

MEDICAL LEGAL RISK IMPLICATIONS OF POPULATION HEALTH MANAGEMENT AND NEEDED CAPABILITIES OF ANALYTICS SYSTEMS

In the near future, there could well be lawsuits from individuals who allege that a healthcare organization's consuming of scarce resources on behalf of one segment of an accountable care population (in which they were members) deprived them (as members of a different segment) of necessary care. Within the population of patients of an accountable care organization (ACO), there could even be class actions by such groups of patients. They might claim that their (highly treatable) healthcare needs were not adequately addressed as a result of decisions made by leaders of ACOs to focus on more "profitable" patients (e.g. certain types of elective surgeries).

To be clinically and financially successful, while minimizing the risk of individual or class actions, the leaders of ACOs will require access to population health management systems to defend their decision making. Population health analytics systems (whether from large firms such as McKesson or Truven Health Analytics, or smaller firms such as MedeAnalytics or Lightbeam Health Solutions) all must possess some common capabilities:

- They should be able to process and analyze extensive and robust data inputs (whether from claims and/or electronically captured and generated from all sources in real or near real time);
- They must be able to produce many different types of clinical process and outcome analyses and meaningful, useful reports. These should include plenty of understandable graphical displays of the care delivered and results achieved at a population, small to large group, and even individual patient level either retrospectively, or in real or near real time;
- They should be able to correlate the clinical process (e.g. the degree of adherence to best evidence based practices) and results (i.e. the full range of patient outcomes) with commensurate financial costs. Doing this will illustrate the resource consumption needed to achieve required clinical results compared to the overall prospectively set budget allocable for particular time periods in contracts with purchasers;
- They should be able to perform highly granular analyses within the populations by patient condition and relative illness severity. These should demonstrate what practice patterns by practitioners for these particular patient groups and subgroups achieve the best clinical outcomes per dollar invested; and
- They should be able to capture these best practices and institutionalize them for the treatment of patients with similar conditions and illness severities coming into the population. This would be the case whether these are new patients or the same patients acquiring or progressing to advanced conditions and illness severities over time. The systems also must facilitate focused continuous performance improvement (through outcomes analytics and real time clinical decision support) of those providers caring for those segments most in need of enhanced care processes and outcomes. Ongoing correlations of clinical and financial outcomes should drive feedback loops producing continuous performance improvement of the entire provider population and determining more accurately what constitutes best practices.

Having in place an operational population health analytics and management system that can achieve the five bulleted functions listed above may not guarantee the avoidance of some of the potential liability situations discussed earlier. However, not having these systems in place will make it very difficult for physicians operating within accountable care organizations to achieve even the Triple, much less the Quadruple, Aim.

ADVANCED DIAGNOSTIC AND THERAPEUTIC DECISION SUPPORT SYSTEMS

We previously covered the breadth and depth of patient safety and risk management considerations of diagnostic and therapeutic decision support systems that are embedded within Electronic Health Records (EHRs). However, presently, there are some systems that are so powerful and advanced in their inner software algorithms, they have not yet been effectively embedded into any particular EHR system. The most notable of these is the IBM Watson supercomputer. Applied to healthcare, this supercomputer's artificial intelligence system has become known as "Dr. Watson". It has been applied to improve the ability of physicians and other providers to determine the most accurate diagnoses, and to advise on the safest and most cost effective treatments. Dr. Watson achieves this by being able to analyze millions of pages of medical information in fractions of seconds.

It will be some years yet before physicians will be required to consult Dr. Watson (or perhaps some even more advanced medical artificial intelligence system) to ensure that they are meeting the applicable standard of care in diagnosing and treating their patients. Nevertheless, IBM recently invested a cool billion dollars to create a division devoted to Watson. Dr. Watson has found that improving the quality, safety, efficiency and value of medical decision making may well be its most important practical application.

The University of Maryland was the first to jump aboard the Dr. Watson bandwagon shortly after Watson annihilated on live television the two foremost human "Jeopardy" champions. Columbia University and the new Cleveland Clinic Lerner School of Medicine soon followed. Leading cancer centers, like Memorial Sloan Kettering Cancer Center, are eying Dr. Watson for its ability to perform comprehensive analyses of genetic markers for different cancers effectively and efficiently. Personalized medicine may soon become the norm in medical treatment (perhaps as early as the middle of the next decade). Look for Dr. Watson (or even some comparable supercomputer coming from Google, Intel or some other high tech company) to become the "go to" technology to ensure the safety and effectiveness of this highly individualized approach to patient management.

In addition to these leading academic health systems, medical schools and cancer treatment facilities, the nation's second largest health insurance company, WellPoint, also began using Dr. Watson recently. Doing so may well impact its many health plans, hundreds of contracted hospitals and tens of thousands of physicians across the country. Executives at WellPoint will assess Dr. Watson's ability to evaluate and continuously improve the performance of its new alternative delivery models at both an individual and population health level. So, the day when hospitals and physicians may be expected to take advantage of this supercomputer's capability to improve their diagnostic and therapeutic decision making and demonstrable patient outcomes may not be that far into the future, after all.

Mobile Health Technologies including Smartphone Apps & Google Glass

The mobile health market is exploding and poised to be a nearly $50 billion a year global industry by the year 2020. The application of mobile technologies to health care (known as "mhealth") promises to democratize and "creatively destruct" the old patriarchal "doctor knows best" culture in American Medicine. Even before practically everyone beyond preschool began using smartphones, the internet and World Wide Web revolution of the 1990s had begun this transformation. The 78 million Baby Boomers never bought into the whole patriarchal view of any social interaction. With the rise of the internet, they began to research and print out reams of information about either their (or, more frequently, their aging parents' or young children's) conditions. Much to their physicians' dismay, they would often present all these printouts at the point of care.

Twenty years later, with smartphones now ubiquitous, members of the even larger 80 million member strong Millennial Generation are (or will soon be) doing the same. They will be doing so not only for themselves, but also (and more likely) for their own aging Baby Boomer parents and young children. Their technologies are considerably more convenient, powerful and portable. They also have much greater proficiency at using them. They will provide the next generation with exponentially greater information in real time at the point of care about illness conditions and their likely course (with or without appropriate medical management). They'll also have estimates of the comparative risks, financial and clinical benefits of a widening range of treatments provided in different settings (including the home) offered by various health plans, literally at their finger (or thumbtips).

In addition to providing instant access to a treasure trove of global medical information, various apps now even permit users to monitor their own health. These monitoring capabilities may already (or soon) include moment-to-moment blood pressure readings, the rate and depth of breathing, body temperature, blood oxygen levels, blood glucose, brain waves, activity, even mood.

[17] *Cf. Topol, How Technology is Transforming Health Care at 3.*

So, for those who are so inclined, smartphones may soon constantly monitor individuals' most important physical and even mental or emotional functioning. This could serve as an endless source of fascination (and probably hypochondria in some). Whole Facebook and Twitter groups comprised of those who are obsessed with their health and daily vital signs, bodily functions and moods could evolve. Their discussions could make hearing about their older relatives' embarrassing health problems over Thanksgiving Dinner seem mild by comparison. We could be creating a generation obsessed with their health beyond what their grandparents' generation ever thought possible.

Even all these new smartphone apps and other mobile health technologies may not be all that distracts even the most focused individuals of this generation. The next big wave is toward mass producing wearable technologies to assist both providers and their patients in monitoring and improving their health. Chief among these is Google Glass.

Google Glass (which makes its wearers look eerily like members of the Borg from "Star Trek" TV shows and movies) is breathlessly being touted as the next big thing in mobile health technologies. A choice few (among them Dr. John Halamka, CIO of the Beth Israel Deaconess Health System in Boston and Co-Chair of the U.S. Health IT Standards Committee) have been wearing Google Glass for some time now. They have been reporting back to Google (and in blogs) on how this technology may be used by Emergency Department physicians (of which Dr. Halamka is one). One such capability is how to obtain and view electronically generated clinical information on patients in real time at the point of care with Google Glasses through voice recognition software.

Surgeons and anesthesiologists may use them to instantly access key information on patients intra-operatively (such as previous X-rays, cardiac angiograms, late breaking lab reports, etc.). Achieving this may not only improve operating room efficiency, but clinical outcomes. Physicians may also share information in real time about the same patient in a hospital (or other treatment facility) to improve care in real time. Below is a commentary on the value of Google Glass (referred to as "Pristine Eyesight" or just "Eyesight") in the operating room by an anesthesiologist:

"Eyesight offers a remote pair of eyes and eyes into that other room. It alerts my pair that something is up and I can immediately look at what he's looking at and determine what to do says Leslie Garson, M.D., Associate Clinical Professor of Anesthesiology at the University of California at Irvine. Since all patient information and images are encrypted until rendered or downloaded (such as the Pristine Eyesight app), these technologies may be fully compliant with federal privacy regulations such as HIPAA. More such Glass innovations are likely to follow, says Henry Lowood, curator of the History of Science and Technology Collection at Stanford University. We're increasingly encountering tech inventions that are open and flexible, he says, noting that Google has facilitated Glass inventions by users via GDK, its Android-based Glass Development Kit."

[32] *Cf. Della Cava, M, Google Glass: Is it a Lifesaver? USA Today; Money 3B; March 3, 2014.*

In what is believed to be a first, the company *drchrono* has recently linked its EHR to Google Glass to produce the first wearable medical record. This wearable medical record is free to users (both providers and patients) on the iPhone, iPad and cloud.

[33] Monegain, B, Google Glass Links to EHR; HealthcareITNews.com (June 19, 2014).

http://www.healthcareitnews.com/news/drchronos-bright-ideas-google-glass.

Mobile Health TechnoLogies-- Impact on the Physician-PatientRelationship and Medical Liability

There may be tremendous potential benefits for using various types of mobile health technologies in achieving (at least) the "Triple Aim" in healthcare delivery. However, just as with electronic records, from a medical legal perspective, there is the real possibility for substantial liability risk. Physicians and other healthcare providers may not be aware of the extent to which their patients may be using (or abusing) these technologies in the name of evaluating and improving their health.

As the great democratizer, mobile health will creatively destruct the "doctor knows best" culture that continues to reign in many, if not still most, parts of American Society even today. In this new world, the best physicians will be team members with their patients and their families. They will also need to function as such with a wide range of healthcare providers in the delivery spectrum over whom they used to claim their ultimate power and influence.

Physicians will need to be teachers and coaches guiding patients and their families as to how to use the ubiquitous and increasingly voluminous (and often conflicting) medical information now instantly accessible. This on demand information may be generated through smartphones, Google Glass, and other, even more sophisticated technologies, yet to be conceived. Physicians will also need to persuade their patients and their families not to get addicted to monitoring their own health to such an obsessive degree that other parts of their lives (including their relationships and their livelihoods) get shortchanged.

Physicians who were trained and grew up in the patriarchal era of medicine will either change or retire. Otherwise, they will become sitting ducks for a new wave of liability actions deriving from this democratization process. Mobile health technologies will dramatically alter the nature of physicians' relationships with patients and their families. Many physicians will be caught unaware concerning the magnitude of these changes or the impact that these will have on how they interact with patients.

Those physicians who do not (or cannot) become the kinds of physicians the Millennial Generation will demand for their own care, and for that of their Baby Boomer parents and young children may find themselves marginalized. If there is any one factor that predicts the likelihood of successful, costly litigation following suboptimal clinical results, it could derive from just such a breakdown in the physician-patient relationship.

As patients and their families pick up more of the tab, they will increasingly expect this kind of equal, collegial, team-based, coaching type of relationship with their physicians. Physicians will need to be able to admit that they don't know everything about what's best for their patients at any given time. This includes not only at the point of care, but, even more importantly, during the 99.9% of their patients' time when they are not in the healthcare system.

Physicians who are unable (or unwilling) to make themselves readily available to their patients and their families through instantly accessible mobile technologies (including texting, e-mail, Twitter, and the like) will also suffer in their relationships with patients. Patients' and their families' expectations of having this instant access will only go up as their proportion of the costs of receiving care does, also. Failure to meet expectations is a second major factor predictor of successful litigation, even when the actual clinical results may not be that bad.

An increasing number of medical liability insurance carriers are now reluctantly admitting the need for physicians (and other healthcare providers and executives) to be ready, willing and able to admit mistakes. They have determined the value of quick and sincere apologies to patients, while also efficiently administering adequate compensation for injuries. Doing this may well be the only way to avoid costly, soul and reputation-crushing litigation publicity. This unwanted publicity may be instantly beamed around the world through various types of mobile health technologies and other social media. Please see more on this "Apology and Quick Compensation" and other new approaches to addressing and resolving medical liability disputes in Chapter 8 below.

The new world of healthcare created by mobile health technologies could well usher in an age of team-based care and unprecedented improvements in public and individual health. On the other hand, those who are not willing to be part of this new order will find themselves marginalized and targets for medical legal ostracism. Younger physicians, particularly those at the vanguard of the Millennial Generation, are much more in touch and in tune with this type of instant communications culture. They are also more comfortable and adept in using mobile technology in both the hospital and medical office practice settings.

It is older physicians (i.e. 55 and older, although this, by no means, is a rule) who may not be quite so comfortable with using these technologies as their younger colleagues, that may be at greatest risk. As a group, they are unaccustomed to serving as a member of a team (unless they are the unquestioned leader). Some may not even believe that these mobile technologies have a rightful place in the context of physician-patient relationships. It is they who are and will be at greatest risk of medical liability as this revolution transforms the practice of medicine and the delivery of healthcare over the next decade or so.

The Mobile Health Era and the Democratization of Healthcare Delivery: The Need for a New Physician Role Model

Older physicians may not necessarily be the best role models for younger physicians at least from the perspective of encouraging completely democratic team based care and technology-facilitated healthcare delivery. Nevertheless, because of their accumulated wisdom (and position in the medical pecking order), they do and will still command a great degree of respect and influence on how younger physicians practice. The best future role models may well be those older physicians, who have changed from being "captains of the ship" to becoming true team-oriented physicians. This new (older) physician role model will have known and overcome the difficulties of becoming comfortable with the new technologies and how they can be used to facilitate both patient/family and extended care team communication. All this may put them in the best position to help younger physician mentees to achieve the Quadruple Aim.

These new physician role models will also need to be more humble about the role of physicians. It is a well-known aphorism that the most expensive piece of technology continues to be the physician's ball point pen (or, more aptly, these days a CPOE system). However, physicians are but one component of a vast multidisciplinary team that makes the delivery of high quality, superior value care possible. Dr. Arnold Relman, the late former Editor in Chief of "The New England Journal of Medicine" and longtime Harvard Professor commented on this. He had just completed his own extended stay at Massachusetts General Hospital (MGH), where he had been treated for a broken neck suffered after a fall in his home, right after his 90th birthday.

Dr. Relman found that the nurses who took care of him were responsible for his ultimate recovery, much more so than were his attending physicians. "I had never before understood how much good nursing contributes to patients' safety and comfort. This is a lesson which all physicians and hospital executives should learn. When nursing is not optimal, patient care is never good."

[34] http://www.nybooks.com/articles/archives/2014/feb/06/on-breaking-ones-neck/?pagination=false

If a physician as revered for the past half century as Dr. Relman can admit that it is nurses, much more than physicians, who make the critical difference in patients' ultimate recovery, then it would seem that physicians of all ages should be able to concede that, also.

Looking ahead, Chapter 7 will focus in more detail about how patient safety and risk management, in conjunction with the new technologies and analytics capabilities, may be used to achieve the Quadruple Aim. Chapter 8 will discuss how the medical liability system, itself, must be transformed to permit achievement of the Quadruple Aim. Chapter 9 will summarize some key takeaways and recommendations. Finally, Chapter 10 (the "Epilogue") will provide a crystal ball picture of how the overall health system will need to evolve in the next 10 years to permit the achievement of the currently elusive goals of the Quadruple Aim.

Chapter 7

NEW METHODS TO PREDICT AND PREVENT MEDICAL LIABILITY ACTIONS

PREDICTIVE MODELING SYSTEMS: THEIR ROLE IN PREDICTING AND PREVENTING LIABILITY WHILE MINIMIZING DEFENSIVE MEDICAL PRACTICES

In similar ways to how predictive modeling systems may be used to project probable medical costs and clinical outcomes of specific populations of patients, so too could these technologies evaluate the relative likelihood of successful medical litigation. The most advanced predictive modeling systems are driven by various types of statistical pattern recognition, heuristic algorithms and/or neural network software analyzing particular combinations of data input.

Data input such as patient conditions and severities, past medical care and results, and/or one of the four most prevalent causes of medical litigation (i.e. communication gaps, medical system defects, suboptimal documentation and/or errors in clinical judgment) could drive these predictive algorithms. They could be used as an early warning system for hospitals and even physicians in their large group practice offices. They could be used to tip off risk managers when the probability of litigation reached a certain threshold of likelihood.

Ethically, these predictions could not in any way be used as a pretext to avoid patients whose encounters made the potential litigation bells start to chime. Nor should physicians use this tool to practice defensive medicine on such patients. Doing this not only increases the costs of care, but also increases the likelihood of patient injury and getting sued, while conferring little clinical benefit. Rather, the value of such a medical liability predictive modeling system would be to make mid-course corrections in patient management before avoidable injuries occurred.

From this author's experience in reviewing hundreds of medical liability cases, it has been the patients who suffered from combinations of poly-pharmacy, multi-testosis and hyperconsultemia who were the most likely to sue. They also were most likely to collect large sums from medical liability insurers through pre-court settlements. Plaintiffs' attorneys and medical experts have been very adept at convincing insurers of how badly in front of judges and juries defendant physicians and hospitals would look. They showcased the uncoordinated, excess testing and invasive procedures of marginal benefit their clients *did* receive (much more often than what care they *didn't* receive). *Defensive medical practices, resulting in patients being afflicted with the conditions of poly-pharmacy, multi-testosis, and hyperconsultemia increase, not decrease, the risks and actualities of successful medical litigation*

It is the wasteful, marginally beneficial, inappropriate, excessive, and ever so costly things that are done *to* patients, not those which are *not* done, which are most associated with successful medical litigation recoveries (most of which are never publicized). These defensive medical practices arise when physicians, hospitals and other providers begin to regard patients as potential plaintiffs trying to hurt them as providers. They begin to regard them less as highly vulnerable people at the most desperate times of their lives reaching out to them at their time of greatest physical and emotional need. A predictive modeling system could be employed to identify these counterproductive patterns associated with defensive medical practice patterns to alert physicians to change course before their physician-patient relationship deteriorated beyond repair.

The other major driver of litigation arises from the failure to meet the expectations that patients and their families have for, if not optimal, at least some kind of improved health results. The more patients and their families are bounced like ping pong balls from one provider to another, the less likely their expectations (whether reasonable or not) will be met. None of these providers (many of whom only see patients once for a procedure or quick examination) have the time to get to know them as human beings well enough. Patients are thrust into the medical testing and consultant-driven invasive procedure gauntlet before this can occur.

What so often results from all this costly, frequently unnecessary, and potentially, if not actually, harmful care is disappointment when expectations of improved health are not met. Indeed, worse clinical conditions and illness severities than before starting this process may well and often do occur.

If insurance cannot cover enough of the humongous medical bill that follows, bankrupting amounts may be passed on to vulnerable patients and their families. This may make suing the only practical (not to mention cathartic) response. By feeding the "more care is better care" mythology, the fee for service healthcare financing system is what ultimately fuels medical litigation. It will continue to be its primary driving force until this nation moves completely away from it to a value based purchasing system of healthcare financing by both the public and private sectors.

Improving Efficiency & Patient Safety: "Choosing Wisely" & Use of a Patient Safety Assessment Tool (PSAT)

Medical Errors: The Breadth and Depth of the Problem

Ensuring patient safety should be one of the best risk management methods to decrease the incidence, severity and success of medical liability claims. Although physicians, hospital executives, attorneys, and even systems engineers have been talking about patient safety for decades, it really didn't become a front burner issue until the Institute of Medicine's landmark report, "To Err is Human".

[28] *Cf. Corrigan, K, et al., To Err is Human; Institute of Medicine; National Academies Press; Washington, D.C. (2000).*

Until that report, at least members of the general public assumed that their safety as patients in hospitals (as well as other parts of the healthcare system) was a foregone conclusion—a "no brainer". But when the IOM concluded in that report that up to 98,000 American patients die needlessly every year due to preventable errors in American hospitals, people far and wide sat up and took notice. This is still the most widely read, reported, publicized and quoted report in the history of the IOM (founded in 1970), if not the entire National Academies of Sciences (started by President Lincoln in 1863 to advise the President, the Administration and the Congress on scientific policy).

Various groups, the American Medical Association (AMA) chief among them, quibbled with the range of 44,000 to 98,000 preventable deaths (believing that the preventable death numbers were probably "only" about 25,000). However, over the past 15 years, other healthcare and patient safety groups have said that the numbers *might well exceed 440,000 per year (10 times the lower of the rate range found by the IOM).* This is the figure estimated by John T. James, a toxicologist at the NASA Space Center who also leads an advocacy group, Patient Safety America.

[35] *James, JT, Scientific-American, Sept. 29, 2013.*

Even more startling, the private sector national quality assessment organization, Health Grades, found in 2011, throughout the United States, *the incidence of harmful, and even lethal, medical errors could well be as high as 40,000 daily!*

[36] *Healthcare Consumerism and Hospital Quality in America Report; Health Grades, 2011.*

Furthermore, Dr Marty Makary, Professor of Surgery at Johns Hopkins, in the "Wall Street Journal" on September 21, 2012, reported that at least 20 to 30% of medications, tests and procedures care are unnecessary and potentially harmful. These could be eliminated while probably *helping*, not harming, patients.

[37] *Makary, M, How to Stop Hospitals from Killing Us; WSJ; Sept. 21, 2012.*

http://online.wsj.com/news/articles/SB10000872396390444620104578008263334441352.

The "Choosing Wisely" Campaign of Medical and Surgical Specialty Societies

The American Board of Internal Medicine (ABIM) Foundation has served as the convener for the "Choosing Wisely" campaign. This campaign has also been supported strongly by the leading medical journal "JAMA Internal Medicine" and its Editor-in-Chief, Rita Redberg, M.D., M.S., Professor of Medicine and Director of Women's Cardiovascular Medicine for the University of California San Francisco (UCSF) School of Medicine. A total of 60 medical and surgical specialty and sub-specialty societies have joined to identify the five most commonly overused and abused tests and procedures in each of their specialties. Their utilization needs to be evaluated much more carefully. Minimizing their use should improve the quality, safety, efficiency and value of healthcare delivery.

[38] http://www.choosingwisely.org.

This campaign to minimize overused and wasteful medical and surgical tests and procedures is linked to the patient safety movement. As analyzed earlier, according to Six Sigma principles, introducing unnecessary complexity into any process increases (perhaps exponentially) the risks and actualities of error and preventable injuries (even when the skill of execution of each step remains the same). Regardless of which numbers to believe (be they as low as 25,000 or as high as 440,000 needless deaths in American hospitals per year due to preventable medical errors), there is a consensus that these numbers are way too high. For something as fundamental as protecting patients from harm in a place (a very expensive place) where the goal is to restore health (not worsen it), *any* number of preventable deaths due to medical error could be regarded as too high!

How can hospitals, health systems, physician groups and other healthcare organizations begin to evaluate their structures, processes and outcomes deriving from them in an effort to minimize these preventable errors? Doing so should improve individual and population health. It should also dramatically improve the safety, quality, and efficiency of care, while also decreasing liability. Is there a systematic way that hospitals, other healthcare organizations and practitioners could undertake to pinpoint those areas where focused patient safety improvement measures and interventions could yield the greatest benefits per dollar invested? Are there tools that could facilitate such assessments and be used as standardized methods for comparing organizations' relative degree of patient safety preparedness to others and to themselves over time? At least one tool that could begin to accomplish that is discussed in the section appearing immediately below—a Patient Safety Assessment Tool (or PSAT).

Using a Patient Safety Assessment Tool (PSAT)

Since patient safety has become of such paramount importance in the modern hospital, it would make sense for them to determine the extent to which they are "patient safety prepared". To determine that state of preparedness, it would also make sense for these organizations to enlist the aid of non-biased third party experts to evaluate the breadth and depth of that preparedness. Otherwise, they're "grading their own paper"—a practice from elementary school which this author always preferred, but which was not exactly fair and accurate.

By so doing, these organizations could then focus on improving those areas of their organizations (be they particular parts, functions, people or technologies or processes) where they could reap the biggest bang for their buck. They could also address situations where there could be potential patient safety time bombs ticking. Achieving this would put them in a much better position to survive and thrive in a post-reform, value based purchasing/accountable care-driven world. It would also protect them from costly corporate liability litigation for not having ferreted out potential or actual safety problems and nipped them in the bud.

A Patient Safety Assessment Tool (PSAT) should be able to evaluate healthcare organizations' preparedness in at least the following areas:

- *Leadership and Strategic Planning* including Physician Leadership and Integration as well as Training in Human Error Recognition and Human Factors Analysis/Engineering;
- *Clinical Leadership and Outcomes Strategic Measures* including Care Coordination through Nursing, Utilization and Care/Case Management, Disease Self-Management and Preventive Programs;
- *Human Resource Development and Training in Patient Safety* including Aviation Style Checklists, Nurse Staffing Ratios based on Patient Acuity, and Intensivist programs and Patient Care Management Programs, etc.;
- *Management of Information Technology and Infrastructure* including the proper use of Computerized Physician Order Entry or CPOE, Technologies to Support Outcomes Management and Real Time Clinical Decision Support as Essential Components of Medical Legal Risk Management, Adverse Clinical Event Tracking Systems, etc.;
- *Process Quality Management and Medication Safety* including establishing common definitions of medication errors to identify, track, reconcile, and eliminate them through an Electronic Medication Administration Record or e-Mar; standardizing adverse drug reactions reporting forms, systematizing data collection/analysis; and providing bar coding to minimize errors;
- *Geriatric Patient Safety* to include geriatric program and nursing assessment, a focus on incontinence as a major source of patient safety problems, fall reduction strategies, skin care assessment and pressure ulcer prevention, use of geriatric consultation services and

specialty units, identification of patients with anemia of chronic disease (ACD), an early warning system for patients with renal insufficiency, risk stratification of patients with chronic kidney disease and monitoring of acute renal failure as a key outcomes indicator;

- *Infection Management and Safety* including the use of antibiotic-impregnated cardiovascular lines and silver alloy urinary catheters and other aids to reduce healthcare-associated infections (HAIs), standardization and development of comprehensive pneumonia management programs especially the appropriate use and timing of blood cultures, antibiotic resistance control practices and use of formularies, screening and administration of influenza and pneumococcal immunizations;
- *Evidence Based Medicine Practices* including, but not limited to, standardization of deep venous thrombosis and pulmonary embolism prevention practices, Warfarin therapy protocols and discharge instructions for patients, nutritional assessments for all medical-surgical patients and those who are critically and/or chronically ill, and assessment of acute abdomens prior to pain management, etc.;
- *Operating Room and Anesthesia Safety* including Aviation Style checklists for patient operating site verification and other fail safe measures, standardization of anesthesia equipment checks and checklists for instrument counts intra-operatively, and the use of guided ultrasound for cardiovascular line insertion, etc.;
- *Process Quality Management and Human Factors Engineering* including development and standardization of physician sign outs and hand offs, standardization of discharge summaries, human-technology interface and operation optimization, and Lean Six Sigma applications; and
- *Quality Management/Patient Safety Results Monitoring* including choosing the right outcomes to be measured and monitored and the role of utilization and case management in patient safety, quality and risk management.

  [39] *Patient Safety Assessment Tool; New World Healthcare Solutions (2003)*

To evaluate the relative patient safety preparedness of all types of healthcare organizations based on the measures listed above, it is important also to employ a standardized scoring methodology. Probably the best for this purpose is one used by the Malcolm Baldrige National Quality Award. This is the only national quality award presented annually by the President of the United States. It goes to applying organizations which are classifiable as large businesses, small businesses, manufacturing and service companies, nonprofit and governmental agencies or healthcare entities. Winners of the Award best meet the hundreds of quality, safety, strategic planning, human resource management, technology deployment, customer service, financial, operating and business performance criteria that comprise the standardized Baldrige Award assessment instrument.

The Health Care Criteria for the Baldrige Award (which this author helped in their initial development in the early 1990s) have now been applicable to applicants since Congress authorized the expansion of the Baldrige Award in 1999. It then was three years (until 2002) before the first healthcare organization won the Baldrige Award. Now, in 2014, there are far more healthcare organizations applying to and winning the Baldrige Award than in any of the other five categories of organizations eligible.

The Baldrige assessment instrument uses a "maturity assessment model" for scoring applicant organizations. This measurement methodology evaluates how far into development and deployment (toward full maturity) organizations are in their various structural, process and outcomes interventions to benchmark and continuously improve quality and business performance. What is important is that organizations can demonstrate that they have thought about, planned for and begun to implement improvement interventions. They need to be able to demonstrate how they have evaluated the relative effectiveness of these interventions. They also must be able to show that they are continually refining these interventions to make them more effective in achieving the ultimate goals of improved quality, safety, efficiency and value to all stakeholders.

The most "mature" organizations have even evaluated (and have an ongoing assessment system in place) that measures the relative maturity and effectiveness of their own self-evaluation methods. In this way, these organizations can ensure that their own self-evaluation methods are accurate, fair and unbiased. They can constantly assess how far along the curve they are in achieving their own quality, safety, efficiency, customer service, value improvement and business performance goals. The PSAT employs all these Baldrige scoring methodologies.

Mimicking the Baldrige Award scoring methodology both as to process measures and outcomes, the PSAT has a "perfect" score of 1000. This score can only be achieved if a healthcare organization can demonstrates itself to be completely mature not only as to its current, but also its future, ongoing development and deployment of all functions promoting patient safety.

No Baldrige Award winner in any of the six organizational categories during the 27 years of the award has achieved this perfect score of 1000. What is important, however, for any healthcare organization (regardless of whether it ever has or plans to apply for the award) is undertaking this process of systematic evaluation. Any healthcare organization can do likewise to evaluate and continuously improve its patient safety preparedness using the PSAT and the maturity assessment model of scoring that the Baldrige Award also employs. Organizations can discover and quantify their strengths and areas for improvement, and then continuously work to enhance their patient safety preparedness over time. In so doing, an organization may benchmark itself by annual or biennial reassessments by the same or a comparable unbiased, expert, third party.

Doing these ongoing patient safety preparedness assessments serve the public health. This is certainly the case since suboptimal patient safety preparedness in this nation's hospitals may well be responsible for up to 440,000 preventable deaths to Americans per year. This makes medical errors the third leading cause of death in America, after cardiovascular disease and just behind strokes.

[35] *Cf. James, JT, Scientific-American article cited above.*

Moreover, in addition to promoting public health, it is certainly in any healthcare organization's enlightened self-interest to be doing this. Improving patient safety will enhance value scores for compensation under new payment models, while minimizing the risks of avoidable litigation. Increasingly, these value scores will be competitive differentiators. The medical legal risk management implications of undertaking ongoing patient safety assessments and using the results to improve will be discussed in more detail in the section following immediately below.

Medical Legal Risk Management Implications of Internal Patient Safety Assessments

Many healthcare organizations might be hesitant to undertake the types of ongoing patient safety assessments described above. Their senior executives might think that a suboptimal score assessed at a time in which their organizations and/or their physicians may have committed an allegedly negligent act would make them a sitting duck. They might fear their defense would be compromised if it ever came out that the very type of detected (or detectable) deficiencies in their safety practices may have been responsible for patient injuries that became the subject of litigation.

However, as discussed previously, there is a well-known exception to the admissibility of evidence in civil litigation like medical liability lawsuits that should protect healthcare organizations in such cases. Evidence of efforts to assess and improve situations to protect the public from harm should not be admissible in actions seeking to show that the very deficiencies sought to be uncovered and eliminated may have been responsible for the alleged harm. Admitting such evidence would dissuade any organization (or individuals within them) from identifying these deficiencies and seeking to eliminate or at least minimize their possible ill effects. Health care providers, quite understandably, would fear that these salutary actions could be used as evidence against them.

This principle often applied in the past to dangerous environmental situations that organizations had sought to address to prevent injuries to the public. However, the same principle could (and certainly should) apply to any situation in a healthcare organization which is seeking to minimize the risks of patient harm. These would include (among many other possibilities): universal precautions to minimize preventable infections, software to minimize the incidence of adverse drug reactions, or any number of hundreds of other safety issues sought to be minimized through specifically designed preventive interventions.

This general rule of evidentiary law was bolstered through the passage in 2005 of the *Patient Safety and Quality Improvement Act (Public Law 109-41).* The Patient Safety and Quality Improvement Act (PSQIA) created a voluntary reporting system in which individuals could anonymously report medical errors, "near misses" or situations of suboptimal patient safety conditions. Through this process, these anonymously reported errors could be analyzed and minimized or eliminated without fear of discovery and use against them (or their organizations). The PSQIA established federal confidentiality protections from discovery for this type of information that may be characterized as "patient safety work product". Breach of this confidentiality protection may result in civil penalties for violators.

The PSQIA also authorizes the federal Agency for Healthcare Research and Quality (AHRQ) to evaluate and list Patient Safety Organizations (PSOs). PSOs are those entities that are qualified under the PSQIA to collect, analyze and report out on the medical errors, "near misses" and other unsafe conditions anonymously and confidentially reported to them. This medical error reporting serves the purpose of ferreting out and minimizing them through specifically designed, targeted, improvement interventions. PSOs are the designated external expert organizations which collect, aggregate and analyze the confidentially protected patient safety work product generated under the PSQIA.

[40] http://www.hhs.gov/ocr/privacy/psa/regulation/

AHRQ lists the patient safety organizations (PSOs) it qualifies under Section 924 of the PSQIA. It also has responsibility for the common formats and network of patient safety databases established through the collection and aggregation of patient safety work product under Section 923 of the Act.

The nonprofit Emergency Care Research Institute, hereafter ECRI Institute or ECRI, applied for and was named as the patient safety organization (PSO) in the state of Pennsylvania. ECRI Institute is a global, private, nonprofit, health services research and technology assessment firm founded by Joel Nobel, M.D., a longtime member of the Consumers Union Board. Dr. Nobel founded ECRI in the 1960s, to evaluate and identify potential safety defects in medical equipment and devices. These were beginning to flood the healthcare marketplace back then. He was motivated to do so when, in 1964, a four year old child died in his arms due to a defective defibrillator.

ECRI's world headquarters remain in Plymouth Meeting, PA (just outside Philadelphia) to this day. ECRI has become the "go to" facility for healthcare organizations around the world to report and work on solutions for minimizing safety problems with medical products. They have had a simulation laboratory at ECRI headquarters for decades to recreate defective products in real life situations. That permits them to pinpoint and eliminate the flaws which could be (and often have been) the source of otherwise avoidable patient injuries. ECRI has also been the only non-university-based Evidence Based Practice Center (EPC), as well as the repository of evidence for the Dept. of Health and Human Services' National Practice Guideline and Quality Measures Clearinghouse (www.guideline.gov) for many years.

Given its many decades' focus on assessing and eliminating medical and healthcare product defects, it was a natural progression for ECRI to move into the broader areas of healthcare quality, patient safety and risk management. It began this progression in the 1980s and accelerated these moves in the 1990s and early 2000s, especially following the publication of the landmark Institute of Medicine report "To Err is Human". ECRI had the technological firepower to collect and to analyze a wide range of medical errors, in addition to its franchise work involved in collecting and analyzing medical and healthcare product safety defects. This positioned ECRI to become one of the first, and, in many ways today, the most prominent and influential, of the PSOs authorized under the PSQIA.

ECRI has been an organization that has focused on evaluating and improving healthcare products for almost a half century. Consequently, ECRI, probably more than any other PSO in the nation, is also in a position to demonstrate how health IT, when used properly, may directly improve care, individuals' and population health, cost containment and medical legal risk management (the Quadruple Aim). In April, 2014 ECRI announced its convening of 10 other PSOs and six professional associations, as well as a group of provider organizations and software vendors, to develop a national framework for proactively identifying and rectifying health IT safety issues—the Partnership for Promoting Health IT Patient Safety. ECRI may also show how health IT may facilitate the comprehensive collection, aggregation, analysis and use of patient safety event data to help design interventions to minimize medical errors, patient injuries, unnecessary costs and avoidable medical liability, in general.

[41] http://www.healthdatamanagement.com/news/Major-New-Effort-to-Unite-on-Identifying-EHR-Safety-Issues-47780-1.html.

ECRI can show how healthcare organizations' patient safety and health IT strategies for development, deployment and continuous improvement can and should be completely aligned to optimize the execution and results of each. The goals of each should be the same, viz. to achieve the Quadruple Aim. Their methods should always be in synch and should mutually feed each other toward achieving shared goals.

ECRI has been and shall continue to be an invaluable resource to the healthcare industry during this all important technology-driven transformation of the health care industry. How ECRI and additional collaborators may predict, prevent and defend against medical liability actions through its role as a PSO and its research into health IT patient safety appears later in this chapter.

The Role of Technology in Medical Legal Risk Management

The old proverb that "an ounce of prevention is worth a pound of cure" could not possibly be more applicable than to medical liability. Once a physician, hospital or other care provider is sued, it doesn't matter if that lawsuit is settled or thrown out the very next day. The damage has already been done. Especially with physicians, they will never be able to look at their patients the same way again. They will see them (at least a little bit) as not just individuals coming to them in a vulnerable state seeking their help, but as potential plaintiffs should things not work out just so.

This perception will promote defensive medical practices by physicians, hospitals and other care providers. As discussed extensively earlier, defensive medicine not only adds substantially to the costs of care directly through the ordering of expensive, unnecessary and/or inadvisable tests, procedures and consultations. These practices also actually increase the risks and actualities of litigation. They undermine the physician-patient relationship, which must remain strong to prevent litigation even in the face of suboptimal clinical results.

As discussed previously, predictive modeling technologies may evaluate what the future costs and severity-adjusted clinical outcomes are likely to be in populations of patients with particular demographics, condition and illness severity mixes. These modeling technologies have computerized algorithms that permit them to process data about patient populations (of varying sizes) to make cost and clinical outcome predictions of what should occur.

These modeling algorithms also may analyze somewhat different information about these same (or comparable) patient populations to predict the likelihood of litigation should current and projected practices continue. This could be an invaluable early warning system risk management tool.

As another example of the capacity of these predictive modeling systems to serve as a medical legal risk management tool, consider the following: Suppose a particular surgical practice was having a higher than statistically expected likelihood of complications (based on demographics, condition and pre-treatment illness severity mix) arising from laparoscopic procedures. The hospital (and/or physician group) could implement proactive, preventive interventions. These interventions could include (among other options):

- Better selection of laparoscopic surgical candidates;
- Better preoperative medical screening of them;
- Better preparation of them including antibiotic prophylaxis;
- Better operative techniques (which could be addressed by more rigorous training requirements and/or better supervision); and/or
- Better immediate and intermediate postoperative care and longer term recovery methods and care.

A good predictive modeling technology should be able to access extensive data from past procedures covering all these pre-, intra-, and postoperative steps in the process. This technology could pinpoint where focused improvement interventions could yield the best ROI. Such a tool could be used to predict and prevent the types of practices and outcomes which could subject the surgeons and the treatment facility (and perhaps others) to the greatest risk of litigation.

A good predictive modeling technology should determine the relative likelihood that specific degrees of deviation from accepted practices and expected severity of illness adjusted clinical outcomes could statistically raise litigation risks. Such a technology should be able to make these calculations to determine if and when (and why and how) a significant revamping of the entire laparoscopic surgical practice for specific types of patients and conditions needed to occur.

This type of advance information could be invaluable to any hospital, health system or even surgical group practice in its planning of technological, operational and human resource development/training and retraining. It could also help significantly in determining whether to continue to market (or, in other ways actively seek or reach out) to particular types of patients as a way of expanding a hospital's or surgical practice's base of patients.

The last thing that any healthcare organization would (or should) want to do would be to market itself to patients as being highly capable of performing procedures, for which they did not have the technological and human resources to deliver optimal care. This would be especially true if an organization's marketing and other methods of communication had led patients to believe that they would be receiving better care than what the organization was equipped to deliver in the face of unexpectedly high volume.

A Technology-Driven Early Warning System to Identify and Prevent Safety Gaps

Another great risk management tool to evaluate and minimize the risks of the use of health IT, itself, is the Health IT Hazard Manager (hereafter, "Hazard Manager"). This was developed through a partnership involving the ECRI Institute, the federal Agency for Healthcare Research and Quality (AHRQ), Abt Associates, and Geisinger Health System's Patient Safety Institute. Recently, ECRI reported data integrity failures in association with the use of Health IT as its Number One Patient Safety Concern for those in the "C-Suite".

[42] http://www.ecri.org/EmailResources/PSRQ/Top10/Top10PSRQ.pdf.

The Hazard Manager now gives all health IT users a central, standardized way to report adverse health IT events and issues. It gives patient safety advocates the ability to compile the data and report the top issues and methods for mitigation with the hope of preventing these side effects from flaring up again.

[43] *Dimick, C, Warning: Health IT may be Hazardous to Your Healthcare; J.AHIMA. March 2014; 88:34-9.*

http://library.ahima.org/xpedio/groups/public/documents/ahima/bok1_050595.hcsp?dDocName=bok1_050595.

"The foundation of the Health IT Hazard Manager is a vendor-neutral health IT hazard taxonomy that allows health IT users and vendors to report specific types of hazards in a standard way. The tool is now being integrated into the non-profit ECRI Institute's Patient Safety Organization (PSO) reporting system, which will collect IT hazards via the Internet and systematically track the root cause of these health IT-related issues."

[43] *Cf. Dimick at 34.*

"Having just launched the tool in October 2013, ECRI will soon issue reports of their findings from the reporting systems that will help health IT users, like hospitals and physicians, as well as health IT vendors manage and prevent issues that arise from their systems. The hope is that the tool can make health IT safer by allowing providers and vendors to fix hazards before they contribute to user error or patient harm, says Karen P. Zimmer, M.D, M.P.H., FAAP, medical director at ECRI Institute PSO."

[43] *Cf. Dimick at 34.*

"The Health IT Hazard Manager aims to identify, record, and track information about a hazard, including:

- What kinds of users encounter the hazard?
- What is the risk of patient harm?
- Who is responsible for fixing the hazard (vendor or provider operator)?
- What steps should be taken to manage this hazard and what is the timeline (turn off the system, monitor, or modify it)?
- Between which products or system interfaces does the hazard occur?

The tool is meant to be used before, during, and after a health IT implementation, and serve as a central place that people from various backgrounds and expertise can learn about hazards. Implementation teams can use it before selecting various health IT systems and during install. Clinicians can use it to identify hazards found while using the systems for care processes. Patient safety teams can use it as they perform root cause analyses when they identify things about health IT they think contributed to a safety incident. Data put into the collection tool can be turned into trend reports that answer important questions about identified hazards, such as:

- What are hazards to watch for with this type of health IT system?
- Is this hazard just happening to one or all providers?
- What is the best practice to solve this hazard?"

[43] *Cf. Dimick at 35*

"According to a recent study by ECRI on health IT-related adverse events, nearly half were human-computer interface issues and the other half was system design issues alone. The goal of the healthcare community should not be to point the finger but to determine the issue and employ human and system changes to ensure the hazard doesn't continue. The approach here is: 'What about the system can be fixed to make it more useable and less error prone?' Walker says. It is less about the blame and shame cycle we get into where we say: 'You made a mistake and we are going to fire you and act like that fixes something.'"

[44] *Walker, Jim, et al., Health IT Hazard Manager Beta-Test: Final Report. Agency for Healthcare Research and Quality; May, 2012.*

http://healthit.ahrq.gov/sites/default/files/docs/citation/HealthITHazardManagerFinalReport.pdf.

"The tool provides ECRI with additional and sharper health IT hazard data they did not previously collect and analyze. Thanks in part to the new tool, in early 2014, ECRI launched a pilot that brings together health IT developers and vendors, health IT practice experts, healthcare industry leaders, associations, and other PSOs to study health IT-related events. Zimmer says this is one of the first times that health IT vendors have partnered with a PSO on health IT hazards. The pilot not only gives all participants broad access to de-identified information on what hazards are being reported to both PSOs like ECRI, but also to other health IT developers and vendors. Prior to the Hazard Manager we collected information on health IT, but now we are able to drill down on hazard specific fields in a structured way to make better sense of the data, Zimmer says."

[43] *Cf. Dimick at 38.*

Medical Legal Risk Management Implications and Significance

The Health IT Hazard Manager, used in conjunction with broader, technology-driven adverse event tracking systems, may represent a quantum leap in the ability of health system and physician organizations in healthcare quality, patient safety and risk management. They may link their systems for tracking ongoing clinical and financial performance results with these adverse event tracking systems.

In doing that, they may demonstrate that identifying and eliminating the root causes of these adverse events (both related to the use of health IT and otherwise) may correlate with continuously improving severity adjusted clinical and financial results. This would be a powerful way to survive and thrive in a value based purchasing, accountable care environment. This could also demonstrate the cost effectiveness of this integrated medical legal risk management system in pursuit of achieving the Quadruple Aim.

EHRs & Big Data Analytics: Their Role in Medical Liability Prediction, Prevention and Defense

The next "Big Thing" in many different industries is so-called "Big Data". Big Data has to do with the ability to harness supercomputing power to analyze and predict through statistical pattern recognition and other means what will likely occur in the future based on what has led to certain trends and events in the past.

Big Data is used by climatologists to try to predict long term future weather patterns based on the analysis of petabytes of information about past weather patterns and what followed after them. Big Data is used by retailers to predict future consumer buying behavior so that they may develop and market products and services ideally even before those consumers themselves recognize that they might need or want them. Big Data is used by all types of scientists to predict the evolution of species and their likely accommodation to rapidly changing environments and ecosystems. Big Data is used by astrophysicists to determine the likely paths of meteors, comets and asteroids to predict their cosmic paths and to ensure that none of them (of a lethal size) are heading in Earth's direction any time soon. The Defense Establishment, Homeland Security and the Intelligence Community also use Big Data to determine where around the world social uprisings and even terrorist attacks (including atomic, biological and/or chemical warfare) may most likely break out.

Given its size, its complexity, its importance socially and economically, and its dependency on using data fully, accurately and appropriately for its effectiveness, Big Data advocates are frothing at the mouth to apply these analytic and predictive capabilities to the healthcare industry. The best estimations are that up to one third of current annual expenditures in the U.S. healthcare system (or a cool trillion dollars annually) could be taken out of the system without hurting, and probably improving healthcare. This provides an unprecedented opportunity for Big Data advocates to demonstrate the value of its investments going into this transformative movement.

There is recent evidence for the value that analysis of large stores of electronically generated data can produce in predicting and preventing mortality and morbidity from septic shock. Septic shock is one of the most lethal and costly conditions occurring to patients in hospitals:

"According to new research, EHRs can be used to predict the early stages of sepsis, one of the leading causes of death in the U.S., responsible for killing some 210,000 people each year. Researchers at U.C. Davis have found that routine health data—blood pressure, respiratory rate, temperature and white blood cell count—from the EHRs of hospitalized patients can detect the illness earlier in its infancy and help pinpoint what patients are at high risk of developing the disease. After analyzing the EHRs of some 741 sepsis patients, researchers were also able to determine that just three measures—lactate level, blood pressure and respiratory rate—can pinpoint the likelihood a patient will die from the disease."

[45] *McCann, E, EHRs may help save lives from sepsis; Healthcare IT News; March 18, 2014.*

http://www.healthcareitnews.com/news/ehrs-may-help-save-sepsis-lives.

"Finding a precise and quick way to determine which patients are at high risk of developing the disease is critically important," said study co-author Hien Nguyen, associate professor of internal medicine and medical director of EHRs at UC Davis, in a March 17 new release announcing study findings.

"We wanted to see if EHRs could provide the foundation for knowing when aggressive diagnosis and treatment are needed and why they can be avoided. The research team is now working on a specific sepsis-risk algorithm that can be automatically calculated in the EHR."

[45] *Cf. McCann above*

The whole Big Data movement has been turbocharged by the conversion from handwritten (often illegible and/or unintelligible) medical records to electronic health records. These may not only be much more readable (and, hopefully, intelligible) by humans, but, as they become more semantically interoperable, also by intelligent machines (i.e. they're "machine readable").

However, at the present time, with relatively few exceptions, that is still more a dream than a current reality. Probably the single biggest obstacle for optimizing the use of electronic health records to achieve the Quadruple Aim in the near term is the continued inability of different proprietary EHRs to be able to transmit and receive electronic communications between and among each other. With the continuing clinical integration of physician practices of varying sizes and specialties into ever merging, larger health systems, there are often literally dozens of non-communicative EHRs that have to be accommodated.

However, the key to using EHRs to achieve the Quadruple Aim is their ability to provide in real time at the point of care complete, accurate and timely information about patients to facilitate optimal clinical decision making by provider and patient alike. So, EHRs continuing inability to do this is not a trivial shortcoming.

The vision of the HITECH portion of the Stimulus Law (the American Recovery and Reinvestment Act of 2009) discussed in Chapter 5 is to have fully interoperable electronic health records. These will permit real time, point of care access to complete, accurate and timely information on patients by providers to optimize their clinical decisions. The three stages of Meaningful Use have been (and continue to be) laboriously developed, critiqued, revised and slowly established as implementation guides. They are intended to incent financially not only hospitals, but especially physicians, to implement and use EHRs that permit this degree of interoperability. However, there has been much pushback on the part of hospitals and physicians (and even EHR vendors and their associations) concerning the criteria to qualify for incentives even under Stage Two, much less, Stage Three. Consequently, the timeline for achieving the vision of HITECH for complete interoperability keeps getting moved further into the future.

Implications of the Continued Lack of EHR Interoperability as a Barrier to the Use of "Big Data"

Until all (or at least a majority of) proprietary EHRs become fully interoperable among themselves, permitting the free flow of secure, private and confidential information on patients to their physicians in real time at the point of care, the vision of HITECH and the Quadruple Aim will not be achievable. In addition, until this free flowing electronically generated patient information may become semantically interoperable and machine readable, the highly touted promise and potential of Big Data in healthcare will also not be realizable. Caregivers must be able to collect, aggregate, analyze and use complete, accurate and timely machine readable data generated from all inpatient, outpatient, clinic, physician and other facilities that patients have frequented across the care continuum over the course of years, or even decades. Only then will Big Data (enabled by widely interoperablel EHRs) be able to facilitate achievement of the Quadruple Aim.

The Role of Clinical Decision Support Systems in Achieving the Quadruple Aim

As discussed earlier, diagnostic and therapeutic decision support systems have been used by physicians and others in healthcare delivery since the 1960s. However, until fairly recently, they remained more the toy of researchers and members of various medical and clinical informatics societies.

With the advent of national healthcare reform, the focus on accountable care and VBP, both diagnostic and therapeutic decision support systems have entered the mainstream in American Medicine. Their appropriate use could begin to eliminate the one third of medical expenditures considered to be wasteful, without hurting (and probably improving) the quality, safety and value of care. These systems, in combination with best evidence based medical standards, could achieve this reduction in waste. They could also help to dramatically decrease the legendary degree of variation in care delivery that occurs across and among different geographies, hospitals, health systems and physician groups.

Nowadays, there are three ways of tapping into the power of these clinical decision support systems: They may be embedded in an EHR (whether or not the user ever activates and uses them as intended—see the previous discussion in Chapter 5 on the medical legal implications of this). They can be passive in nature (requiring the physician or other user to actively engage them to become available for use). Alternatively, they may be thrust upon physicians and others, requiring them as users of the EHR to actively disengage them (or to ignore them, if that is possible without more forcefully turning them off). These clinical decision support systems (or CDSS) are driven by built in inference engines that interface with the electronically generated data from the EHR. They may function on the basis of statistical pattern recognition and/or different types of neural network technologies to produce their intelligence-based guidance.

Another way by which to engage CDSS is through their tight integration with either an Electronic Prescribing or Computerized Physician Order Entry (or CPOE) system. In this way, these systems' inference engines and "if then" logical algorithms may provide ways of dissuading physicians from ordering certain medications or other treatments which might be contraindicated, or could otherwise interfere adversely with the intended effects of other treatments.

CDSS may also be purchased and/or used separately from the EHR. However, for them to be optimally effective, they would be dependent on receiving electronically generated data from the EHR and from all other sources of data (electronic or non-electronic) on patients. These therapeutic decision making systems may be characterized as:

- *Feedback class* providing feedback to actions taken by physicians or others such as alerts on allergies, drug-drug interactions, parameter checking looking for dosing errors and redundant (i.e. duplicate) testing;
- *Data organization* providing aggregate data trending for key indicators for large numbers of patients over time (e.g. to detect the emergence of antibiotic-resistant patterns);
- *Proactive information* (e.g. best evidence based pathways in the treatment of specific conditions, such as pneumonia, congestive heart failure, heart attacks, etc. at different points along the care continuum);
- *Intelligent actions* (e.g. rule based event detection actions to follow such as checking blood glucose levels in patients with hyponatremia, or time based checks when expected transactions have not occurred, such as a warfarin order not being filled by a specific time);
- *Communications* alerting physicians and other providers who need to know about unusual data (via automated e-mails); and

- *Expert advice* to reduce uncertainty in the interpretation of tests and other information (which can provide probability estimates of particular conditions in patients based on demographics and the most recent results of tests and other currently available information).

[46] *Cucina R. Chapter e4. Information Technology in Patient Care. Citing: Papadakis MA, McPhee SJ, Rabow MW. eds. CURRENT Medical Diagnosis & Treatment 2014. New York: McGraw-Hill; 2014. http://accessmedicine.mhmedical.com/content.aspx?bookid=330&Sectionid=44291048*

Risk Management Implications from the Use of CDSS—Areas for Interdisciplinary Research

As rapidly increasing percentages of physicians and other providers begin to use the various types of CDSS, researchers at academic health systems need to conduct retrospective studies to discern what types of patterns of use (or nonuse) of CDSS are correlated with patient injuries that either do (or do not) result in litigation. They should undertake these analyses to evaluate which types of alerts and other means of modifying clinical decision making behavior actually improve the quality, safety and value of care, and which may not (by increasing liability risk).

These types of studies can and should be undertaken with academic health services researchers, clinical epidemiologists, biostatisticians and health information technologists. These professionals should also be joined in their efforts by in house lawyers, quality, patient safety and risk managers and outside counsel and medical liability insurance professionals. The results of such research could provide tremendously valuable guidance for EHR and CDSS software developers in the years and decades ahead as they and their users seek to achieve the Quadruple Aim.

Chapter 8

How Must the Medical Liability System Change for the Quadruple Aim to be Achievable?

Shortcomings of the Current Medical Liability System

The most common refrain heard from physicians when told of the Quadruple Aim is that the lawyers (both those representing plaintiffs and defendants) won't let them achieve all four goals. They claim that they always must be vigilant about not failing to order enough tests, procedures and consultations. Otherwise, one of them they didn't order may have revealed conditions in patients, which, if not treated in a timely fashion, might result in what could and should have been avoidable injury and litigation.

It is true enough that in the context of our current medical liability system, there is a danger of getting sued for not having diagnosed and treated certain conditions (especially cancers) in an accurate and timely fashion. However, this potential reality should not drive clinical decision making. What should drive decisions is the assessed pre-test *probability*, not the conceivable *possibility,* that an otherwise undiagnosed condition (of whatever severity) could be revealed by the timely execution and accurate interpretation of a particular test or procedure.

Still, the current medical liability system will need to be changed, and probably transformed, just as thoroughly as the overall healthcare system needs to be. The liability system needs to avoid penalizing this more rational (and less fear and defensive-based) approach to clinical decision making (by providers and patients alike). By generating fear on the part of even the most rational physicians that missing an obscure condition in a patient could result in a career-threatening lawsuit, the current medical liability system is highly counterproductive. It does not help physicians or other providers to achieve the Quadruple (or even the Triple) Aim. A by-no-means-exhaustive list of the shortcomings of the current medical liability system would include the following (but not be limited to):

- *The current medical liability system is highly unpredictable* when it comes to assessing which cases are likely to generate large verdicts or settlements and which will not. Juries (and even non-medically trained or experienced judges) may have entirely variable opinions and draw strikingly different conclusions. They may differ widely on what type of evidence should carry more or less weight in finding liability and the extent of compensable damages.
- *The current medical liability system may not result in accurate, or even fair and unbiased expert opinions* in its approach to bringing cases from start to finish. Cases first need to be evaluated by medical experts on the plaintiff's side before they go forward. Unfortunately, in many cases, these medical experts are the same ones used by specific attorneys on an on-going basis. They may very well not be the most qualified to evaluate the medical merits of specific claims. They may even have a built in conflict of interest if their determining a case should go forward might result in more financial gain for them down the road.
- *The current medical liability system is extremely labor intensive, cumbersome and time-consuming.* Cases may take from two to three years (from the time they are filed) to be resolved by either verdict or settlement. That is just an (optimistic) average. That is on top of the time between when the allegedly negligent incident occurred (or was discovered) and the case was filed (usually just inside the statute of limitations period). This period may be lengthened even further in cases where the injury (such as failure to detect cancer or some other condition) may not be discovered (or be "reasonably discoverable") for years. With infants, toddlers, children and youth, the statute may not even start running until they reach majority age status. All this results in tremendous costs to the parties and the overall system, given all the evidence and document discovery, depositions, expert reports,

motions, pre-trial preparations and briefings that may be generated. It also puts patients and their families (not to mention defendants and their families) in a highly distracting, often agonizing, "Legal Limbo" for years, or even decades. Although usually used in the context of criminal trials, the time-worn phrase--"Justice delayed is justice denied"—is just as applicable (for both parties) in medical liability suits.

- *The current medical liability system feeds the practice of defensive medicine* (as analyzed extensively in previous chapters above). It can make even the most compassionate physician less concerned about addressing a patient's medical and quality of life needs, and more worried about constructing a sufficient shield against possible liability actions. These defensive medical practices prevent even the "Triple Aim", let along the "Quadruple Aim" from getting accomplished. By regarding patients as potential plaintiffs, rather than individuals seeking their help at very vulnerable times, physicians seriously jeopardize the quality of their all-important relationship with their patients. This relationship, not defensive medical practices, is the most powerful "shield" from liability that physicians possess.

Any transformed medical liability system, which not only will not be an obstacle to achieving the Quadruple Aim, but may actually be a facilitator of it, must address these shortcomings. The following sections discuss three options that have been proposed to accomplish this goal. There have been other proposals over the past 40 years since the first medical liability crisis in the middle 1970s. Some of these others have either been discarded, or have become variants or components of those consolidated into the three options appearing below.

THE APOLOGY APPROACH

Even the thought of ever saying "I'm sorry" at any time after (or before) a medical liability action was launched used to send shivers up the spine of even the most easy going defense attorneys (especially hospital counsel). In the traditional medical liability system, saying "I'm sorry" is tantamount to an admission of liability and all the damages that would follow. The sentiment is that for a physician, of all people, ever to admit a mistake, it must be a whopper.

But why do patients become plaintiffs? They feel powerless, abandoned and betrayed. They may come to regard suing as the best (if not only) route to gain back some degree of control, or even dignity (not to mention the money to pay all their medical and other bills). Their healthcare providers' refusing to admit that things may not have gone exactly as intended, may create more than enough anger to turn patients into plaintiffs. All other factors remaining equal, if their providers had not stonewalled, it is more likely that patients would not have become plaintiffs in the first place.

The University of Michigan Health System was one of the first major healthcare organizations in the country to evaluate in a systematic way whether this type of an approach to risk management might actually decrease liability exposure. Since 2001, the University of Michigan Health System has had an "Apology and Offer of Compensation" policy in place for alleged medical errors. Researchers conducted a retrospective analysis to determine if the rate and costs of medical liability claims decreased with the institution of this policy.

After full implementation of an apology-with-offer policy, the monthly rate of new claims dropped from 7.03 to 4.52 per 100,000 patient encounters. The average monthly rate of lawsuits dropped from 2.13 to 0.75 per 100,000 patient encounters. Median time from claims reporting to resolution decreased from 1.36 to 0.95 years. Average monthly cost rates dropped by 59% for total liability and patient compensation costs and by 61% for non-compensation legal costs.

[47] *Kachalia, A, et al., Liability Claims and Costs Before and After a Medical Error Disclosure Program; Ann. Intern. Med. 2010; August 153(4):213-21.*

http://www.annals.org/article.aspx?articleid=745972.

As a result of this study and its dramatic results, as of the time of this writing, there were 37 states that now have in place some type of Medical Apology legislation. It is expected that this number will continue to increase, and perhaps even give rise to bipartisan national legislation in the foreseeable future.

No Fault Medical Liability Legislation

The big difference between this alternative to the current medical liability system and the Apology and Compensation approach is that with "No Fault", there is an explicit recognition that no fault has been assigned (or is even assignable). This is unlike the Apology and Compensation legislation. The act of apologizing does not admit to fault or negligence. However, doing so does not eliminate the notion that there might have been fault on the part of somebody or something which resulted (in a medical and legal sense) in the patient's claimed injuries.

No fault in medical liability actions follows the model (with appropriate modifications) used in automobile and workers' compensation insurance systems. The common thread is to remove what might otherwise be highly litigious, cost and time-consuming disputes from the traditional tort system.

The No Fault option is one that has been advocated by the Common Good (which has also been a chief advocate of specialized health courts discussed below). The Common Good is a high level group of experts in medicine, law, public health and policy that has focused on finding ways to rationalize our legal system to take out much of its unnecessary cost and hassle. The Common Good has often joined with the Robert Wood Johnson Foundation as its sponsor, and with the Harvard School of Public Health as a research collaborator in its work.

"Replacing medical malpractice lawsuits with a no-fault system could offer broader compensation of injured patients while changing medical providers' attitudes and behavior in confronting medical errors. Designers of such a system face a difficult task in reconciling the competing values and needs at stake. Striking a balance too far in the direction of relieving providers' litigation burdens could result in patients losing not only the unique form of agency they wield in tort litigation, but also some of their awards. In order to ensure that consumers benefit from a no-fault project, some basic protections must be built in:

- Initial review of claims should be made by an independent entity rather than an insurer-dominated entity and each claim should be reviewed separately by more than one expert.
- If at least one expert reviewer is convinced that a patient's injury was preventable, the claim should proceed to a full hearing with that expert's opinion admitted for consideration.
- If the demonstration project participant pays out less in compensation than it would have expected to pay under the (current) tort system, the differences in funds should not be retained by the provider or insurer unless an evaluation of the project reveals a decrease in the error rate.

In other words, there should be no incentive to manipulate the system to reduce net payouts.

- Any pilot or demonstration project should be conducted under governmental auspices and public supervision; it should not be created solely by contract with patients or purchasers."

[48] *Williams, J, No-Fault Medical Malpractice Compensation: Policy Considerations for Design of a Demonstration Project; AARP; Washington, D.C. (2007).*

http://assets.aarp.org/rgcenter/health/2007_06_malpractice.pdf.

No-fault may be an appealing approach to the current unpredictable, highly adversarial medical liability system on the one hand. On the other hand, medical liability litigation may be much more complex than either automobile or even workers' compensation actions. Without all the safeguards noted above, taking medical liability litigation out of the tort system could raise constitutional issues concerning whether plaintiffs (and perhaps even defendants who wanted their names cleared) have been denied their "day in court". That is why, even more persuasively, the Common Good has been advocating at state legislatures, and, even at the level of the U.S. Congress, the alternative of specialized health courts. A discussion of those follows.

Specialized Health Courts

Specialized health courts (analogous to tax and bankruptcy courts) have been a celebrated cause of Philip Howard, Esq., Senior Partner at Covington & Burling, LLP and Founder and Chairman of the Common Good, for at least the past dozen years. He has spoken of the urgent need for specialized health courts recently to help to remove the trillion dollars of annual waste in the current American Healthcare System. In his blog from March 10, 2014 entitled: *Affordable Health Care Requires a New Legal Framework,* Mr. Howard's points follow below:

"There are three major structural causes of unaffordable health care in America. One is defensive medicine (3-10% of total costs), caused by unnecessary tests and procedures done in part to help protect doctors from possible lawsuits for not 'doing enough.' Second, is the "fee-for-service" reimbursement system, which incentivizes providers to provide more (not better) care, accounting for an estimated 20 to 30% of extra cost. The third is bureaucracy—a torrent of bureaucracy—that invades every nook and cranny of caregivers' days, costing twice as much per capita as the next most bureaucratic state, or an extra 15% of the healthcare dollar on excess administration. Doctors spend over 20% of their time on what used to be known as paperwork.

None of these sources of waste is a secret. The drafters of Obamacare tried to deal with aspects of them, as Ezekiel Emanuel recounts in his new book, *Reinventing American Health Care (Cf. Ref. 18, above)* But change is hard. Change scares people. Change disrupts special interests. When things are working really badly, anarchist Peter Kropotkin observed at the turn of the last century, people cling even harder to the status quo, 'lest [change] may make him more wretched still.'

Change happens, but typically when the old system collapses. Wasting a trillion dollars a year on inefficient health care—that's about $10,000 per family—will eventually cause the branch to break. So what should the new system look like?

Solving these problems requires entirely new frameworks. Fee-for-service systems should be replaced by "accountable care organizations," in which a provider takes care of all of a person's health needs for one annual fee. When a patient needs specialized care, it should be done as 'bundled payments', basically a fixed fee for everything to do with that problem.

Defensive medicine is the area of waste that Common Good is trying to solve. What's needed is clear: replace unreliable jury-by-jury verdicts (and years-long emotionally-charged proceedings) with expert health courts that reliably sort good care from bad care. Only then can doctors go through the day relying on their best judgment instead of listening to a little lawyer on their shoulders.

The Obama administration and Dr. Emanuel have been helpful in advancing the cause of reliable healthcare justice; for example, in 2011 Obama presented a budget that included $250 million to help fund medical justice reform initiatives, including special health courts. I met and spoke with Dr. Emanuel several times during his tenure as a key healthcare adviser.

But Dr. Emanuel is not accurate in suggesting that the Affordable Care Act advances the cause of reliable justice. Yes, early drafts of the Act included provisions for pilot projects of alternative systems of justice. But Senate Majority Leader Harry Reid is a champion of trial lawyers. In the law as enacted, these pilots are permissible only if they 'provide patients the ability to opt out of or voluntarily withdraw from participating in the alternative at any time.'

Keeping the jury, of course, eviscerates the whole idea of consistent decisions. One jury can decide a case one way; another jury on the same facts can decide exactly the opposite way. Most studies suggest that an expert court would be fairer for injured patients as well as more reliable for innocent doctors. But the Affordable Care Act is unwilling to countenance a pilot project that doctors could rely upon.

President Obama's heart certainly seems to be in the right place on this issue. But it will take more than a suggestion to an obdurate Senate to advance this reform. The public, polls show, overwhelmingly supports special health courts. But no change is likely to happen until there's firm leadership from the President, or a crisis."

[49] *Howard, P, Affordable Health Care Requires a New Legal Framework; March 10, 2014.*

http://www.commongood.org/blog/c/health-care.

For further evidence of the magnitude of the costs of defensive medicine that could be averted through specialized health courts, please see this study by Dr. Michelle Mello and her team. As a Professor at the Harvard School of Public Health, she has worked very closely with the Common Good in alternative medical dispute resolution research.

[50] *Mello MM, Chandra A, Gawande AA, Studdert DM. National costs of the medical liability system. Health Aff. (Millwood). 2010;29(9):1569-1577.*

Specialized health courts may provide assurances to physicians and other providers that they will not be subject to the unpredictable whims and vagaries of non-medically trained and experienced juries and judges. They will also provide incentives for physicians and other providers to seek out and follow the latest evidence based medical practices. These will be the vehicles through which medically trained and experienced judges will determine whether or not there is a justiciable claim by plaintiffs that may be brought in the traditional court system.

Proponents of specialized health courts will need to ensure that they are not being used as insurmountable barriers for plaintiffs (and even defendants) from getting their "day in court". No-fault systems will need to have such safety valves, also. Specialized health courts are not intended to interject yet another layer of bureaucracy in the entire medical dispute resolution process. They are designed to provide some degree of accuracy, predictability, fairness and dispatch in the whole process of determining whether or not there is a meritorious case based on the evidence and applicable law.

The nation will evolve rapidly in the years and decades ahead into much more of a technologically-driven, transformed health care system. Medical liability litigation will only get more complex to be able to prove. It will become even more difficult for plaintiffs to be able to recover damages for legitimate injuries that would likely not have occurred but for there being a demonstrable breach in the standard of care. So, there will be definite benefits for patients, also, to be able to go through a specialized health court system with medically trained and experienced judges. Going this route will permit them to get more predictable, and much speedier and less expensive to the system, adjudications and recoveries (where warranted). This will prevent them from having to rely upon the current medical liability system which functions more like a lottery. Certainly, physicians and other providers will be in a much better position to be able to pursue and achieve the Quadruple Aim in a more forthright and confident manner than what they presently can with the current medical liability system.

Chapter 9

CONCLUSION

SUMMARY

This nation's $3 trillion, completely fragmented, mind numbingly complex, grossly inefficient, terribly error prone, and often unjust healthcare financing and delivery system is on the brink of transformation to move away from what has become an otherwise financially unsustainable course. Admittedly, the rate of healthcare inflation has slowed during the past few years significantly (either as a result of the Great Recession and/or the Affordable Care Act). However, with the recovering economy and the addition of millions of previously uninsured people through the ACA, healthcare inflation once again is likely to be on the march soon. More importantly, with 78 million Baby Boomers rapidly entering their years of greatest healthcare expenditures, dramatic changes will still be required.

Failure to act quickly to move from a volume to a value based system will result in multi-trillion dollar federal deficits in the 2020s, exhaustion of funds for the Medicare Hospital Program, widespread medical bankruptcies, and the inability of American companies to compete globally. As a nation, we will need to determine how to achieve much better clinical results and quality of life factors most important to those receiving the care. We will need to be able to conduct these analyzes on defined populations of patients. The providers for these populations will receive predetermined amounts of money periodically allocated by major public and private sector healthcare purchasers (governments and employers). How well providers can demonstrate that they can achieve the Quadruple Aim will determine the extent to which they receive these funds.

Health insurers will continue to play a role in this transformed healthcare system. However, they will become primarily generators, collectors, aggregators, analyzers and producers of data for reports on populations of patients' conditions and illness severities. They will use this information on behalf of their remaining public and private sector healthcare purchaser customers to evaluate current and projected healthcare costs based on patient populations' past illness and injury trends and genomic mix. They will do these analyses to provide real time guidance on how much it should cost to manage the healthcare needs of patients and their families to achieve optimal clinical results per dollar invested.

Needless to say, the latest information technologies designed to permit these types of "Big Data" analyses comprehensively, accurately and as near to real time as possible will be essential. So too will be that all the data generated on individuals and populations may be collected, aggregated and analyzed after being standardized and normalized utilizing uniform formats and coding nomenclatures.

There will need to be so-called "semantic interoperability" among all of the various electronic health record, e-prescribing, computerized physician order entry, and clinical decision support systems. Hospitals, health systems, physicians and every other type of provider delivering care to patients along the continuum will need to be able to collect complete information on patients as near to real time as possible at each point of care. This will be necessary for them to optimize clinical decision making. To be truly informed in their clinical decision making, physicians and all other direct providers of care increasingly will require the input of patients and their families after sharing with them the latest information about their conditions, genetic susceptibilities, and illness severities. This will include the latest and most accurate information about their diagnostic and therapeutic options, their risks, benefits and out of pocket financial costs to them based on their particular health plans' offerings.

Providers on all segments of the care continuum will need to be able to access in near real time at the point of care the latest and most complete information about their patients' conditions and illness severities, including that's monitored through a whole host of mobile health devices. They will also need to be able to run this information through the latest computerized diagnostic and therapeutic algorithms of leading edge clinical decision support systems. Intelligent and appropriate use of these will be essential for physicians and other providers along the care continuum to be able to optimize the demonstrable health status and quality of life of their patients within increasingly tighter financial constraints.

By achieving demonstrably superior value in the treatment of their assigned population of patients, new healthcare organizations (comprised of combinations of hospitals, health systems, physicians and other delivery component facilities) will see their accountable care, bundled payment and/or medical home/neighborhood contracts renewed. Healthcare organizations unable to demonstrate the superior value of the care they deliver will lose their contracts.

There still may be something resembling current fee for service practice in rural areas and other chronically underserved areas. However, in all those areas in which there will be physicians and other providers competing to take care of populations of patients, what is described above will become the norm. Once the so-called "Cadillac Tax" kicks into high gear by the end of the current decade, it remains to be seen how many employers (of whatever size) will shunt their employees into the health insurance exchanges. If as much of that occurs as some experts have predicted, we truly will have a consumer-driven healthcare system. Even before that occurs, such a system is already rapidly coming to pass, as employers continue to pass an increasing proportion of the costs to patients and their families through more high deductible plans and other means.

MEDICAL LEGAL IMPLICATIONS OF THIS TECHNOLOGY-DRIVEN TRANSFORMED HEALTH SYSTEM

The overarching theme of this book has been how not only to accomplish the Triple Aim of better health, improved care and lower costs, but also the Quadruple Aim. The Quadruple Aim includes the fourth goal of decreasing the risks and actualities of medical liability. A recurring emphasis has been that the technology needed to transform to a value-based healthcare system is a double edged sword: It holds great potential if used appropriately, but medical legal peril, if not.

How to survive and thrive in a value-based healthcare system to achieve all four goals of the Quadruple Aim is covered immediately below in the "Recommendations" section. That will be followed by an Epilogue (Chapter 10), which envisions what a technology-driven, transformed healthcare delivery and financing system, capable of achieving the Quadruple Aim might look like by the middle 2020s.

RECOMMENDATIONS

Any type of change (even when for excellent reasons) increases the opportunities for and actualities of errors. This is true in any field of endeavor. However, in a $3 trillion industry that has more than 14 million workers in it that have grown accustomed to doing things in very specific ways, the odds are that any change (no matter how necessary and ultimately beneficial) will exponentially increase those risks.

The mere introduction of new information technologies, alone, even when intended to decrease the risks and actualities of errors, may dramatically increase the risks and actualities of errors and harm. This is especially true in an area as personalized and already fraught with risk as healthcare is. Add to that mix all the changes in the organization, delivery and financing of healthcare through bundled payment arrangements, medical homes and neighborhoods, and accountable care organizations, whose name alone may increase the risks of medical liability.

The recommendations appearing below may just seem like common sense. That is an accurate, but not sufficient observation. In the rush to tick off all the boxes to demonstrate their "meaningful use" of electronic health records to gain their share of the tens of billions of dollars ponied up by the federal government, providers have taken many shortcuts. That's only human nature. At the same time, many hospitals, health systems and physician groups are jumping headlong into all the new types of healthcare delivery and financing organizations. They may well not really understand what it will take to successfully manage the health and financial risk of defined patient populations for whose care and costs they are willing to become accountable. This could undermine the whole purpose for implementing these new delivery and financing vehicles, and the information technologies enabling them, in the first place, i.e. to achieve the Quadruple Aim.

Taking those caveats into account, appearing below is a "Top Ten List" of the key recommendations for navigating the uncharted waters of healthcare reform and the implementation and use of the technologies required to keep their ships afloat. These would include (but not be limited to) the following:

- All providers must truly understand what it means to be accountable for taking care of the health needs of specific populations of patients for discrete periods of time and for predetermined amounts of money;
- Assuming that a clinically integrated entity, or CIE, comprised of a hospital or hospitals, a physician group or groups, and some type of payer (or risk-bearing provider) decides to take on population health risk, it must be prepared to deliver and finance care in very different ways than previously;
- Before engaging in risk-bearing, members of a CIE must have in place the information and process execution infrastructure to collect, aggregate, analyze and report on the demographics, condition and illness severity mix of the populations under their care. They must be able to predict how to manage their patients' health and costs to meet both clinical and financial outcome expectations of the ultimate underwriter of that care;
- Members of clinically integrated entities (CIEs) need to be at least as aware of what goes on with patients when they are not in front of them, as when they are. It is during the 99.9% of the time that patients aren't in front of their providers that their health results are most impacted;
- All providers must become conversant with and be willing to communicate with their patients in nonconventional ways including social media (assuming their patients' consent to have medical information communicated through this format);
- All providers must be aware of the extent that their patients track their health status indicators through the many different devices and mobile phone apps now becoming available to do so;
- Members of CIEs (and especially physicians who are either in a CIE or not) will need to work much more as team members with other providers who have specific roles in managing their patients and impacting their outcomes. They will also need to function as team members with patients and their families. Not doing so will not only result in suboptimal outcomes, but also failures to meet their patients' expectations. This will significantly increase the chances for litigation even when their outcomes may be the best achievable under the circumstances;
- Members of CIEs (and especially physicians who are either in a CIE, or not) will need to be conversant with and communicate to patients

and their families information about the costs of care, just as much as they do about its clinical benefits and risks. This will become increasingly necessary as more of the ultimate costs of care are borne by patients and their families. This will be especially the case with the growing number of high deductible plans purchased both through the exchanges and as included as part of employee benefits offerings;

- All providers (but especially those in CIEs) must understand the capabilities and limitations of the information technologies necessary for their practices to function effectively. They need to understand that any capability of a system that is overridden or ignored, carries substantial liability risk should injury occur to patients which, more likely than not, would not have occurred, had the capability been used; and
- All providers must be prepared to be constantly evaluated by those who receive and pay for the care that they deliver. They must be willing to be part of ongoing continuous performance improvement initiatives. They must be willing to change their practice patterns and other behaviors to continuously improve the individual and population health status of their patients. All providers (but especially physicians) must be willing to serve on teams (as leaders, but, more commonly, as "just" members). They must be able to produce improvements in the health of their patients, by demonstrating the ever better quality and cost effectiveness of their care delivery, and their abilities to minimize medical liability risk—i.e. accomplishment of the goals of the Quadruple Aim.

Chapter 10

EPILOGUE: ACHIEVING THE QUADRUPLE AIM IN THE NEXT DECADE AND BEYOND

Bill Gates, Founder of Microsoft, has said (to paraphrase): "We usually overestimate what can be accomplished in one year, but underestimate what can get done in 10 years." That has certainly been true with many technologies of the past several decades (e.g. the personal computer, the internet, the smartphone and other electronic gadgets). However, this has not rung true (so far) for electronic health records, many of their embedded diagnostic and therapeutic decision support systems, and other types of health information technologies.

Some of those technologies (e.g. electronic health records and decision support systems) have been out there for nearly a half century (at least among academicians and other researchers). Many of the pioneers of these systems (e.g. Drs. William Stead of Vanderbilt, Larry Weed of Case Western and the University of Vermont, Octo Barnett of Harvard and Perry Miller of Yale, among others) would probably agree with the following conclusion: Even today, at least in the U.S., those in the healthcare industry have not realized the vision for these technologies (i.e. to achieve at least the Triple, if not Quadruple, Aim) to a much greater extent than when they first began to design these systems for that very purpose *several* decades ago.

What have been the reasons for such slow technology penetration (or at least value realization) in the $3 trillion healthcare industry? Providing a comprehensive list of these reasons would fill another chapter. However, three of the most important reasons have been the following:

- The fee for service reimbursement system has insulated most in the industry from needing to be terribly efficient. This has protected much of the 14 million strong in healthcare, which may be the biggest employer in many, if not most, communities, from the usual market forces. In healthcare, it truly is the case: "*One man's waste is another man's treasure*";
- The highly fragmented third and fourth party methods by which payments to providers occur, has made demonstrating electronic health information technologies' value and ROI (benefiting which party is not even clear) in any systematic and standardized manner well-nigh impossible; and
- There has been a great suspicion among healthcare workers "of a certain age" (especially physicians) about the value of electronic health information technologies. Many believe (with some justification) that they depersonalize the all-important relationship they have with their patients and their families, as well as disrupt their well-oiled clinical process workflows.

What will likely change in the next decade to overcome these three obstacles that have prevented electronic health information technologies from being drivers (rather than potential impediments) for achieving the Quadruple Aim?

Clearly, the biggest of these changes which needs to occur is the one most entrenched because of the many benefits it has conferred on so many for so long. That is the conversion from a volume to a value based compensation system. It has become blindingly obvious that fee for service is primarily responsible for so many of the current problems in the healthcare system. However, changing it to what would be a much fairer, higher quality, safer and efficient value-based system brings to mind the old analogy of trying to get a battleship to make a U-Turn in a bathtub.

Nevertheless, the incessant debate over healthcare since the 2008 Presidential Campaign has finally gotten a critical mass of bipartisan policymakers to recognize that fee for service is unsustainable as a financing model. In June, 2014, the Chairman of the powerful U.S. Senate Financing Committee, Ron Wyden, (D-OR) said that he wants to "….take a machete to the fee for service system." This transformation may be driven or facilitated by the government and/or by the private sector (both of which recognize their key economic stakes in changing this system). Regardless, within the next 10 years, we will have moved decisively from a volume to a value based model.

The continued viability of our long term economy and global competitiveness will demand that this occur.

As the move to a value based system hastens, so too will the extremely fragmented healthcare system become much less so. This will occur from economic necessity. To compete effectively for value based contracts, hospitals, physicians and others will have to band together to pool sufficient resources. This consolidation will also permit them to have access to the capital necessary to acquire and retain the technologies required to demonstrate the superior value of their care delivery to those who receive and pay for their services. For probably the first time, it will begin to be possible to demonstrate the relative value and ROI of advanced technologies (and other investments). These technologies will be evaluated by how well they support highly integrated systems of hospitals and physicians (and all the other provider components across the care continuum) to become clinically and financially successful in a value-driven marketplace.

Finally, there will be an inevitable "changing of the (old) guard" that will accelerate over the next 10 years and beyond. The median age of physicians (and many other of the 14 million healthcare workers in this country) should drop steadily over the next decade and beyond. A big part of this will be as a result of physicians in the 78 million-strong Baby Boomer Generation (born between 1946 and 1964) trading in their stethoscopes for golf putters (or shuffleboard sticks). Although there are always exceptions to any rule, this retirement boom will likely remove disproportionately those physicians (and other healthcare workers) who have been most resistant to the information technology revolution in healthcare.

At the same time, there will be a rapidly growing influx into the healthcare industry (not just of physicians but of all healthcare workers) of card-carrying members of the 80 million-strong Millennial Generation (born between 1980 and 2000). Members of this huge demographic group are highly comfortable and conversant with the latest in information technologies. The Great Recession has left many of them unemployed or underemployed. This youngest adult generation is (and will be) desperately seeking meaningful employment in a vibrant, and still rapidly growing, industry like healthcare. Healthcare will continue to have plenty of jobs that can (and will) need the unique capabilities of those who are the most up to date in their knowledge and skills concerning how best to use the latest in information technologies to help achieve the Quadruple Aim.

INDEX

J

K

L

M

N

O

P

Q

R

S

T

U

V

W

Y

Z